D0975526

THE
ELEMENTS
OF
INVESTING

THE
ELEMENTS
OF
INVESTING

Easy Lessons for Every Investor
Updated Edition

Burton G. Malkiel
Charles D. Ellis

Preface by Gus Sauter
Foreword by David Swensen

WILEY
John Wiley & Sons, Inc.

To our delightful grandchildren,
Porter, Mackie, George, Jade, Morgan,
Charles, and Ray

CONTENTS

Contents

Contents

PREFACE TO UPDATED EDITION

At her death in 1999, at the age of 91, Oseola McCarty bequeathed $150,000 to the University of Southern Mississippi. For her generosity, she received an honorary degree from the university and the Presidential Citizens Medal, the second highest civilian award in the United States. Her gift was all the more extraordinary because she earned her living washing clothes.

At a very young age, Ms. McCarty was taught by her mother to be a great saver. She made tradeoffs, spending what she needed to live on, but forgoing any luxuries. She had a used TV, but only watched shows that she could pick up over the airwaves. She did not own a car, electing to walk everywhere. She lived in a house that she inherited from her uncle. Over the course of her lifetime, she amassed a remarkable nest egg, estimated to be about $250,000.

Ms. McCarty was the very model of a disciplined saver. Her example shows that a little bit of will power—and yes, thrift—can add up to big things. This is Lesson No. 1 in any sound financial plan, and it is Lesson No. 1 in this wonderful book by Burton G. Malkiel and Charles D. Ellis.

Over the past several decades, Malkiel's *Random Walk Down Wall Street* and Ellis's *Winning the Loser's Game* have helped millions of people to understand the fundamentals of investing and to reach their financial goals. In *Elements of Investing*, Malkiel and Ellis distill their wisdom and experience into a sensible plan for people to save and invest.

Some money managers warn that successful investing can be carried out only by the most sophisticated and talented professionals. And, of course, these managers claim to be members of that small club. Malkiel and Ellis argue that successful investing should not be the province of a select few. Football games are not always won by the best quarterback. They are won in the trenches. Investors have to win the war of blocking and tackling.

Elements of Investing provides a road map that can multiply your savings to reach your financial target. It starts with understanding the answers to some basic questions, like when will you need this money? And how well can you tolerate investment risk? The answers to those questions can help you build an appropriate asset allocation between stocks, bonds, and cash.

It should be a balanced approach, and the investments should be broadly diversified. Most importantly, the authors stress that the investments must be low cost. One certainty about investing is that, for a given return, the more you spend to earn it, the less of it you will keep. The authors conclude that the best way to implement your plan is to invest in low-cost index funds.

This approach is certainly not sexy. Blocking and tackling is not sexy. But, I daresay that most investors would be better off if they followed this strategy. Indeed, it's the kind of approach that we espouse at Vanguard. It has served many clients very well over the years.

This updated edition of *Elements of Investing* brings a clear-eyed perspective to the current environment, including a new chapter describing the aftermath of the global financial crisis, and its impact on the way people are rethinking their approach to investing. Pundits bombard us with claims that the old rules no longer apply. They say that we are in a protracted environment of low returns and high volatility, and that people should abandon buy-and-hold investing and become more opportunistic. Malkiel and Ellis take umbrage with these claims, and at Vanguard, so do we.

The authors reaffirm the views they expressed in the first edition and they provide supporting evidence. Diversification, rebalancing, dollar-cost averaging, and low-cost indexing remain the best path to achieve investment success.

This book is a must-read for all investors—those new to investing and those who have been at it for a while. It should be required reading in high school because the power of compounding is particularly valuable at a young age. But veteran investors will also benefit from reading this book as it debunks many misconceptions and identifies behavioral biases that stand in the way of successful investing. And, just to make sure you do not fall prey to the siren's song of a better way, you should reread this book every several years.

Over the course of my career, I've seen time and again how the simple principles discussed in this book have helped ordinary people achieve extraordinary results.

George U. "Gus" Sauter
Chief Investment Officer, Vanguard
October 2012

FOREWORD

In *The Elements of Investing*, Charley Ellis and Burt Malkiel, two of the investment world's greatest thinkers, combine their talents to produce a remarkable guide to personal finance. Having already written two of the finest books on financial markets, Ellis's *Winning the Loser's Game* and Malkiel's *A Random Walk Down Wall Street*, why should the authors revisit the subject of their already classic volumes? The sad fact is that in the cacophony of advice for individual investors, few sane voices are raised. In writing *The Elements of Investing*, the authors provide an important service to the lay reader, honing their message to the bare essentials by heeding Albert Einstein's dictum that "everything should be made as simple as possible, but not simpler."

Investors have three tools to deploy in the portfolio management process—asset allocation, market timing, and security selection. Asset allocation involves setting long-term targets for each of the asset classes in which an investor invests. Market timing consists of short-term bets against the long-term asset allocation targets. Security selection deals with the construction of the asset classes that an investor chooses to employ.

Ellis and Malkiel correctly focus on asset allocation since asset allocation accounts for more than 100 percent of investor returns. How can it be that more than 100 percent of returns come from the asset allocation decision? Market timing and security selection involve significant costs in the form of management fees paid to outside advisors and commissions extracted by Wall Street brokers. Such costs ensure that investors will underperform by the totality of investment management costs, which represent transfers from investors to their agents. Hence, the expensive activities of market timing and security selection reduce the returns available for the community of investors and that is the reason asset allocation explains more than 100 percent of investor returns.

Ellis and Malkiel observe that investors consistently make perverse market timing decisions, chasing hot performers and dumping laggards. Study after study of mutual fund trading concludes that investors buy high and sell low, subtracting value with their timing decisions. Ellis and Malkiel sensibly advise investors to adopt a coherent long-term strategy and stick with it.

Security selection decisions further reduce returns. Ellis and Malkiel cite depressing statistics regarding the failure of the majority of mutual fund managers to exceed the returns of low-cost, passive, market-matching index strategies. The documented dismal numbers only begin to capture the enormity of the situation. Ellis and Malkiel cite numbers only for funds that survived, a relatively successful subset of the mutual fund universe. The failures, which as a group produced miserable returns, are nowhere to be measured. Many funds disappeared. The Center for Research in Security Prices collects data on all mutual funds, dead or alive. As of December 2008, the Center tracked 39,000 funds, only 26,000 of which are active. The 13,000 failed funds do not show up in the authors' studies of past returns because the failed funds do not have current track records. (They disappeared, after all.) Considering the experience of mutual funds, dead and alive, reinforces Ellis and Malkiel's advice to take the low-cost, passive approach.

Of course, even in a slim volume, quibbles arise. I view home ownership more as a consumption good and less as an investment asset. I cast a skeptical eye on Ellis and Malkiel's implicit endorsement of stock picking in their confessions regarding personal success in security selection. (Is it surprising that two of the greatest figures in modern finance would figure out how to beat the market? Yes, they can pick stocks—the rest of us cannot.) I more emphatically recommend Vanguard, which, along with TIAA-CREF, operates on a not-for-profit basis and thereby eliminates the money management industry's pervasive conflict between profit motive and fiduciary responsibility. Quibbles aside, *The Elements of Investing* delivers an important and fundamentally valuable message.

When I was a doctoral student at Yale in the late 1970s, my dissertation advisor, Nobel laureate James Tobin, suggested that I read *A Random Walk Down Wall Street* to learn about how markets really work. Burt Malkiel's wonderful book provided a critical foundation for my academic work. When I returned to Yale in the mid-1980s to manage Yale's endowment, I came across *Investment Policy*, the predecessor to *Winning the Loser's Game*. Charley Ellis's marvelous volume informed my approach to investment management in countless ways. Now, Charley Ellis and Burt Malkiel have produced a magnificent primer on investing for all of us. Follow their recommendations and prosper!

David F. Swensen
Author of *Unconventional Success: A Fundamental Approach to Personal Investment*
Chief Investment Officer, Yale University
July 2009

INTRODUCTION

In 104 years of study and experience,* here are the Elements of Investing we wish we'd always known. Experience may well be the best teacher, but the tuition is very high. Our objective is to provide individual investors—including our delightful grandchildren—the basic principles for a lifetime of financial success in saving and investing, all in 208 pages of straight talk that can be read in just two hours. There are many good books about investing. (Indeed, we've even written a few ourselves.) But most investing books run to 400 pages or more and go into complex details that tend to overwhelm normal people.

---

*54 for Burt and 50 for Charley.

If you're like most people, you have neither the patience nor the interest to plow through that much detail. You want to get the main things right. Still, having unbiased information about financial decision making and avoiding costly investing errors is critically important.

That's why we present the most important lessons in this easy-to-read, jargon-free little book. If you happen to be familiar with William Strunk Jr. and E. B. White's classic book *The Elements of Style*, you will recognize one of the original sources of inspiration for this book—and why we are so brief. If you are unfamiliar with Strunk and White, don't worry. All you need to know is that they whittled down the art of powerful writing to a few basic rules of usage and composition. In less than 92 pages, they shared *everything* about writing that truly mattered; brevity and precision became instant virtues. Strunk and White's wafer-thin classic has chugged along for decades. No doubt it will outlive us all.

We now dare state our goal on the equally important topic of investing. How surprising to us that *everything* of importance on such a heady topic can be reduced to rules you can count on one hand. Yes, investing can be that simple if your brain remains unclouded with taxing complexities. These rules will truly *make a difference*.

Our promise: Reading this book will be the best time you could spend to put yourself on the right path to long-term financial security. Then, over your lifetime, you can pick this book up again to scan its lessons and remind yourself what is elemental if you want to turn a loser's game into one you can really win.

IT ALL STARTS WITH SAVING

This is a short, straight-talk book about investing. Our goal is to enhance your financial security by helping you make better investment decisions and putting you on a path toward a lifetime of financial success and, particularly, a comfortable and secure retirement.

Don't let anyone tell you that investing is too complex for regular people. We want to show you that everybody can make sound financial decisions. But it doesn't matter whether you make a return of 2 percent, 5 percent, or even 10 percent on your investments if you have nothing to invest.

So it all starts with saving.

It doesn't matter whether you make a return of 2 percent, 5 percent, or even 10 percent on your investments if you have nothing to invest.

I

SAVE

Save. The amount of capital you start with is not nearly as important as organizing your life to save regularly and to start as early as possible. As the sign in one bank read:

> *Little by little you can safely stock up a small reserve here, <u>but not until you start.</u>*

The fast way to affluence is simple: Reduce your expenses well below your income—and Shazam!—you *are* affluent because your income exceeds your outgo. You have "more"—more than enough. It makes no difference whether you are a recent college graduate or a multimillionaire. We've all heard stories of the schoolteacher who lived modestly, enjoyed life, and left an estate worth over $1 million—real affluence after a life of careful spending. And we know one important truth: She was a saver.

But it can also go the other way. A man with an annual income of more than $10 million—true story—kept running out of money, so he kept going back to the trustees of his family's huge trusts for more. Why? Because he had such an expensive lifestyle—private plane, several large homes, frequent purchases of paintings, lavish entertaining, and on and on. And this man was miserably unhappy.

In *David Copperfield*, Charles Dickens's character Wilkins Micawber pronounced a now-famous law:

> *Annual income twenty pounds, annual expenditure nineteen pounds nineteen and six, result happiness. Annual income twenty pounds, annual expenditure twenty pounds ought and six, result misery.*

Saving is good for us—for two reasons. One reason for saving is to prevent having serious regrets later on. As the poet John Greenleaf Whittier wrote: "Of all sad words of tongue and pen, the saddest are 'It might have been.'"* "I should have" and "I wish I had" are two more of history's saddest sentences.

Another reason for saving is quite positive: Most of us enjoy the extra comfort and the feeling of accomplishment that comes with both the *process* of saving and with the *results*—having more freedom of choice both now and in the future.

No regrets in the future is important, or will be, to all of us. No regrets in the present is important, too. Being a sensible saver is good for you, but deprivation is not. So don't try to save too much. You're looking for ways to save that you can use over and over again by making these new ways *your* new good habits.†

The real purpose of saving is to empower you to keep *your* priorities—not to make you sacrifice. Your goal in saving is not to "squeeze orange juice from a turnip" or to

---

* This line is from a poem entitled "Maud Muller," written in 1856.
† Or as Malcolm Gladwell suggests in *Blink*, you might try to get taller. Being six feet tall adds over $5,000 a year to your income because our society prefers taller people—so they enjoy better-paying careers.

make you feel deprived. Not at all! Your goal is to enable you to feel better and better about your life and the way you are living it by making your own best-for-you choices. Savings can give you an opportunity to take advantage of attractive future opportunities that are important to *you*. Saving also puts you on the road to a secure retirement. Think of saving as a way to get you more of what you really want, need, and enjoy. Let saving be your helpful friend.

FIRST DO NO HARM

The first step in saving is to stop *dis*saving—spending more than you earn, especially by running up balances on your credit cards. There are few, if any, absolute rules in saving and investing, but here's ours: *Never, never, never take on credit card debt.* This rule comes as close as any to being an inviolable commandment. Scott Adams, the creator of the Dilbert comic strip, calls credit cards "the crack cocaine of the financial world. They start out as a no-fee way to get instant gratification, but the next thing you know, you're freebasing shoes at Nordstrom."

Credit card debt is great—but not for you (or any other individual). Credit card debt is great for the lenders, and only the lenders. Credit cards are a wonderful convenience, but for every good thing there are limits. The limit on credit cards is *not* your announced "credit limit." The only sensible limit on credit card debt is *zero*.

Credit card debt *is* seductive. It's all too easy to ease onto the slippery slope—and slide down into overwhelming debts. You never—well, almost never—get asked to pay off your debt. The bank will "graciously" allow you to make low monthly payments. Easy. Far too easy! Your obligations continue to accumulate and accumulate until you get The Letter, saying you have borrowed too much, your interest rate is being increased, and you are required to switch, somehow, from money going *to* you to money going *from* you to the bank. You are not just in debt, you are in *trouble*. If you don't do what the bank now says you must do, legal action will be taken. Be advised! Never, never, never use credit card debt.

START SAVING EARLY: TIME IS MONEY

The secret of getting rich slowly but surely is the miracle of compound interest. Albert Einstein is said to have described compound interest as the most powerful force in the universe. The concept simply involves earning a return not only on your original savings but also on the accumulated interest that you have earned on your past investment of your savings.

> The secret of getting rich slowly, but surely, is the miracle of compound interest.

Why is compounding so powerful? Let's use the U.S. stock market as an example. Stocks have rewarded investors with an average return close to 10 percent a year over the past 100 years. Of course, returns do vary from year to year, sometimes by a lot, but to illustrate the concept, suppose they return exactly 10 percent each year. If you started with a $100 investment, your account would be worth $110 at the end of the first year—the original $100 plus the $10 that you earned. By leaving the $10 earned in the first year reinvested, you start year two with $110 and earn $11, leaving your stake at the end of the second year at $121. In year three you earn $12.10 and your account is now worth $133.10. Carrying the example out, at the end of 10 years you would have almost $260—$60 more than if you had earned only $10 per year in "simple" interest. Compounding *is* powerful!

THE AMAZING RULE OF 72

Do you know the amazing Rule of 72? If not, learn it now and remember it forever. It's easy, and it unlocks the mystery of compounding. Here it is: $X \times Y = 72$. That is, X (the number of years it takes to double your money) times Y (the percentage rate of return you earn on your money) equals . . . 72.

Let's try an example: To double your money in 10 years, what rate of return do you need? The answer: 10 times $X = 72$, so $X = 7.2$ percent.

Another way to use the rule is to divide any percentage return into 72 to find how long it takes to double your money. Example: At 8 percent, how long does it take to double your money? Easy: nine years (72 divided by 8 = 9).

Try one more: at 3 percent, how long to double your money? Answer: 24 years (72 divided by 3 = 24).

Now try it the other way: If someone tells you a particular investment should double in four years, what rate of return each and every year is he promising?

Answer: 18 percent (72 divided by 4 = 18).

For anyone whose attention is attracted by the Rule of 72, the obvious follow-on is surely compelling: If a

10 percent rate of return will double your money in 7.2 years, it will double your money again in the next 7.2 years. In less than 15 years (14.4 years to be exact), you'll have *four times* your money—and *sixteen times* your money in 28.8 years.

So if you're 25 and you skip one glass of wine at a fancy restaurant today, you might celebrate with your spouse the benefit of compounding with a full dinner at that same restaurant 30 years from now. The power of compounding is why everyone agrees that saving early in life and investing is good for you. It is great to have the powerful forces of time working for you—24/7.

Time is indeed money, but as George Bernard Shaw once said, "Youth is wasted on the young." If only we could all train ourselves at a young age to know what we know now. When money is left to compound for long periods, the resulting accumulations can be awe inspiring. If George Washington had taken just one dollar from his first presidential salary and invested it at 8 percent—the average rate of return on stocks over the past 200 years—his heirs today would have about $8 million. Think about this every time you see Washington on a U.S. dollar bill.

Benjamin Franklin provides us with an actual rather than a hypothetical case. When Franklin died in 1790, he left a gift of $5,000 to each of his two favorite cities, Boston and Philadelphia. He stipulated that the money was to be invested and could be paid out at two specific dates, the first 100 years and the second 200 years after the date of the gift. After 100 years, each city was allowed to withdraw $500,000 for public works projects. After 200 years, in 1991, they received the balance—which had compounded to approximately $20 million for each city. Franklin's example teaches all of us, in a dramatic way, the power of compounding. As Franklin himself liked to describe the benefits of compounding, "Money makes money. And the money that money makes, makes money."

A modern example involves twin brothers, William and James, who are now 65 years old. Forty-five years ago, when William was 20, he started a retirement account, putting $4,000 in the stock market at the beginning of each year. After 20 years of contributions, totaling $80,000, he stopped making new investments but left the accumulated contributions in his account. The fund earned 10 percent per year, tax free. The second brother, James, started his own retirement account at age 40 (just after William quit) and continued depositing $4,000 per year for the next 25 years for a total investment of $100,000. When both brothers reached the age of 65, which one do you think had the bigger nest egg? The answer is startling:

- William's account was worth almost $2.5 million.
- James' account was worth less than $400,000.

William's won the race hands down. Despite having invested less money than James, William's stake was over $2 million greater. The moral is clear; you can accumulate much more money by starting earlier and taking greater advantage of the miracle of compounding.

We could run through dozens of other examples using actual stock market returns. One investor might start early but have the worst possible timing, investing at the peak of the stock market each year. Another investor starts later but is the world's luckiest investor, buying at the absolute bottom of the market every year. The first investor, even though she may have invested less money and had the worst possible timing, accumulates more money.

Luck in picking the right time to invest is all well and good, but time is much more important than timing. There is always a good excuse to put off planning for retirement. Don't let it happen to you. Put time on your side. To get rich surely you have to do it wisely—which means slowly—and you will have to start now.

Like all financial tools, the Rule of 72 needs to be applied wisely. It's great when it's working for you but ghastly when working against you. That's what makes credit card balances so dangerous. With credit card debt, 18 percent is the "normal" interest rate charged. And if you don't pay promptly, you'll soon be paying interest on interest—and interest on the interest on the interest.

Credit card debt is the exact opposite of a great investment. Wouldn't you like to have an investment that compounded at such a rapid rate? Of course you would. We all would. At 18 percent, a debt doubles in just *four* years—and then redoubles again in the next four years. Ouch! That's four *times* as much debt in just eight years—and it's still compounding! That compounding is why banks have distributed credit cards so widely to people they don't even know. And that's why you should never *ever* use any credit card debt.

SAVVY SAVINGS

We can hear the chorus of complaints already: "I *know* that the only sure road to a comfortable retirement is to spend less than my income. I *know* that regular savings is the key to building wealth, but I can't make ends meet as it is!" In this chapter, we offer you some help by presenting a number of savvy savings tips. Still, success will be up to you.

Saving is like weight control. Both take discipline and both depend on the right framing—the right way of thinking about the discipline. Start with a single and powerful insight: People who are thin *like* being thin, and people who save *like* saving. For many, the key to successful saving is to see saving as a game, a game of control where you put yourself in control and make the important choices even though your world is filled with thousands of daily temptations.

In both saving and weight control, successful people concentrate their thinking on the *benefits* they will enjoy. Savers take pleasure in being savers and in having savings just as weight watchers take pleasure in being thin, looking their best, receiving compliments, being in good health, and knowing they'll enjoy longer lives. Savers enjoy the inner satisfaction of being in control of their finances and knowing they are ensuring their own financial independence and future happiness.

Warren Buffett, widely regarded as the world's greatest investor, is famous for modest personal spending even though he counts his net worth in the tens of billions. To Buffett, a dollar spent early in his life costs him $7, $8, or more—the amount that dollar would have become over time if he had invested it.

Because they center their thinking on enjoying the benefits of achieving their goals, most savers and most slim people take pleasure in the *process* of saving and the *process* of keeping trim. They do not think in terms of deprivation; they think in terms of making good progress toward achieving their goal. As they make progress toward their goal, they have the fun and satisfaction of achievement.

You can, too.

The secret to saving is being rational. Being rational is simple, but by no means easy, because we're all so human and are hard wired to be flawed as savers and investors. For most of us, the best way to start being more nearly rational is to discuss the topic openly and honestly with one or more good friends. This works best if your friend is your spouse because he or she is as important to you as you are to her or to him and, of course, you depend on each other.

If, after candid discussion, you like what you see about your spending, that's really great. Carry on! However, if like most of us you notice some things you do that you don't like, think of these "misses" as invitations to do better.

The easiest way to save is to skip all impulse purchases. Make up a shopping list *before* you go to the store and stick to your list. This will help you stay focused on figuring out not only *what* you do with your money, but *why.* Practice "double positive" shopping when you and your spouse or friend go together: Agree that nothing gets purchased without both of you saying yes.

Saving provides you with the extra money you can use to make your future better. Learn by self-observation how you could increase your success rate on spending wisely *and* on saving. The goal is clear: Get the most of what *you* really want out of *your* life.

Every month or two, go over your expenditures, including credit card charges, together. Did each expenditure give you equal value for money? Were they all equally worthwhile to you? Probably not. Now focus on the most questionable few. Could you have had as much fun or memories as good without one or two of them? Could you have quite happily substituted an alternative?

Do you ever get talked into spending more than you meant to by friends or salespeople or advertisements? Have you *never* been showing off—not even a little? Since almost all of us are influenced by what we see our peer group doing, chances are high that you are influenced, too. So take a little extra time to decide for yourself.

Here's an easy test of whether you are being influenced by what your neighbors will think: If you were the only person who would ever know, would you spend the money? Keeping up with the Joneses and the Smiths, as we all know, is a powerful force for spending. We like to be like our friends. Teenagers are not the only ones who dress the way "everyone" dresses. That's why brands like Prada, Givenchy, and Polo are so valuable.

Take a careful look at all your expenditures and "triage" them into three baskets—best value, good value, and dubious value. Then look for a few that, on reflection, are not really of high value to you. Then stop them from taking your money away from you! Drop that money into a jar, or a bank, just as a squirrel saves acorns for winter.

If you stayed in a smaller, plainer hotel room, would you really care? If a superior room is worth it to you, fine.

17

But if not, you have an opportunity to save and direct your savings to something you really do care about.

For some city dwellers, taking a subway is better than finding a taxi because it is a lot cheaper and often faster. For others, a taxi is worth the extra expense. And some people—each with one of those two different kinds of preferences—are happily married to each other. Their secret is to agree to disagree and to set limits.

One of us loves fine wines, knows a lot about them, and has a substantial collection. He "shops" the wine list in a restaurant for value and almost always orders a superb wine at a bargain price. He gets great joy from the selection process *and* from drinking the wine with dinner. The other never drinks any wine. To each his own. Both are happy campers.

There are small ways to save and there are big ways to save. Let's list some of each.

SMALL SAVINGS TIPS

Here are some ways to save on a few "little things," but they can be fun and they do add up:

- Buy Christmas cards on December 26 or 27—for next year.

- If you're out for dinner, find the two dishes you like best and order the less costly one and pocket the difference. Or consider ordering a second appetizer—often "starters" have the best flavors—and pocket even more.
- Instead of going out to the movies, rent a recent release from Netflix, make your own popcorn, and drink what's in your refrigerator.
- Buy books—even current best sellers—secondhand on Amazon.com.
- Set the thermostat a few degrees lower in winter and wear a sweater.
- Exchange your morning $4 latte for a simple cup of coffee.
- Keep a record of all your expenditures. You'll likely find that you really don't need a lot of things you are now buying.
- Take the change out of your pockets each day and put it into a piggy bank. It can eventually add up to a vacation. Or at the end of each month, put the funds into an investment plan.
- Shop for low-cost auto insurance—and a further discount if you have a good driving record.

- Next vacation, think of a fun place that is nice but out of season.

BIG WAYS TO SAVE

Here are some big ways to save. These *really* add up:

- If you feel you need life insurance, buy inexpensive term insurance sold by local savings banks or available on the Internet.

    Term life insurance rates have been going down because people are living longer, insurance companies are better at segmenting customers by risk, and the Web is cutting the cost of distribution. (Check out Term4Sale.com and Accuquote.com.) Ten years ago, the "standard" man at age 40 paid $1,300 for 20-year $100,000 term life insurance. Today he pays only $600. Nice savings.

- Concentrate your investments with low-fee managers. We will show you later what the low-fee investment products are and how you can get them.

- Buy nearly new pre-owned cars or use a smaller car—or both.

- Self-insure small and moderate risks by having high deductibles on your auto insurance or fire insurance. Much of the cost of insurance is paperwork on numerous small claims. Chances are, you can self-insure on most losses and really only need insurance against major problems that are unlikely.
- Cut your spending back to what you were spending two or three years ago.
- Ask your employer to help you save by automatically deducting 5 percent or 10 percent of your weekly pay and adding it to your tax-advantaged investment account. If you pay yourself first, you'll pay less in tax and be less likely to spend every nickel you earn.
- Enroll in a "Save More Tomorrow" plan. These plans commit you to save some part—and only part—of next year's raise.

Think in terms of opportunity cost. Think of every dollar you spend as the amount it could grow into by the time you retire. Ben Franklin famously advised, "A penny saved is a penny earned." He was right but not entirely right. The Rule of 72 shows why. If you save money and invest it at, say, a 7 percent average annual return, $1 saved today becomes $2 in about 10 years, $4 in 20 years, and $8 in 30 years, and so on and on, inevitably growing. So the dollar a young person spends on some nonessential today would mean that $10 or more will be given up in retirement.

If you need further discipline, remember that some say the only thing worse than dying is to outlive the money you have set aside for retirement.

LET THE GOVERNMENT HELP YOU SAVE

Throughout history, people have changed their behavior to avoid taxes. Centuries ago, the Duke of Tuscany imposed a tax on salt. Tuscan bakers responded by eliminating salt in their recipes and giving us the delicious Tuscan bread we enjoy today. If you visit Amsterdam, you will notice that almost all the old houses are narrow and tall. They were constructed that way to minimize property taxes, which were based on the width of a house. Consider another architectural example, the invention of the mansard roof in France. Property taxes were often levied on the number of rooms in a house and, therefore, rooms on the second or third floor were considered just as ratable as those on the ground floor.

But if a mansard roof was constructed on the third floor, those rooms were considered to be part of an attic and not taxed. So follow the historical tradition. Tax minimization should be a key objective in the way you organize your financial life. And by minimizing taxes, you can have more to save and invest.

We are not suggesting that you attempt to cheat the government. Don't even begin to think of that. But we do urge you to take full advantage of the variety of opportunities to make your savings tax deductible and to let your savings and investments grow tax free.

In the United States, consumers have long lived beyond their means; consumption expenditures have been excessive, savings inadequate, and indebtedness dangerously high. As a matter of national policy, a number of tax incentives have been established to encourage Americans to save. *But millions of Americans are not taking advantage of these incentives.* For all but the wealthiest people, there is no reason to pay any taxes at all on the earnings that you set aside to provide for a secure retirement. Almost all investors, except the super wealthy, can allow the earnings from their retirement investments to grow tax free. We describe the vehicles available to you in the Appendix at the end of this book.

OWN YOUR HOME

"Neither a borrower nor a lender be," declared Polonius in Shakespeare's *Hamlet*. As usual, Shakespeare had it right—almost. As with every good rule, there's one exception: a mortgage on your family home. While we believe you should never take on credit card debt, a mortgage makes sense for four reasons:

1. It enables a young family to have a nice place to live when the kids are growing up.
2. Your bank will not let you borrow more than you can sensibly handle given your income. (This was true for 70 years. Then, as we've recently painfully learned, banks lent too much and we have all suffered the global financial crisis. Now sensible mortgage lending is going to be the rule again. Thank goodness!)
3. A mortgage is a very special kind of debt: When you take out a mortgage, *you* decide when to pay the money back. (Being in debt is different. When you're in debt, as in credit card debt, the *lender* decides when you have to pay it back. That decision can come your way at a

most inconvenient time.) And remember the tax advantages of owning a home financed with a mortgage. The mortgage interest costs are tax deductible, so Uncle Sam helps out by lowering your tax bill.

4. The rate of interest you will pay on a home mortgage is *substantially* below the interest rate on credit card debt.

The price of homes has risen along with inflation for more than 100 years, so housing usually has been a good inflation hedge. Of course, that wasn't the case during the great real estate bubble of 2006–2008, but house prices have now returned to more normal values and home ownership is once again a sensible investment in family happiness.

HOW DO I CATCH UP?

"Okay, coach," you might say at this point, "I wish I'd read your book when in my twenties. But I didn't begin to save, or get out of debt, early in life. Now, in my fifties (or even sixties), I have little or no accumulated savings. Is there *any* way to close the money gap?"

Fortunately the answer is yes, and Uncle Sam provides some extra tax incentives to help you catch up. But it won't be easy. The only way to make up for lost time is to start a disciplined program of saving—*now*. The tax laws make it possible for investors over 50 to make extra contributions to their tax-advantaged retirement plans. By making additional contributions to employer-sponsored 401(k) or individual retirement plans, older investors can reduce current taxes and ensure that all of the earnings from their investments accumulate tax-free.

While there are lots of uncertainties as you look forward to retirement, one thing is certain: By spending less, you can save more—and saving more is essential. It's never too late to downsize your current lifestyle and start saving. You could consider selling your large house and moving into a simpler, less expensive place. Or you could move to a less expensive location where living costs and taxes are lower. You don't have easy choices, but with discipline you can make up for lost time.

You may decide to push back your retirement date a few years. There's no law that says age 60, 65, or even 75 is the particular age at which you should stop working. Indeed, people who work at least part-time into their seventies are generally healthier and more alert than those who do nothing. And postponing retirement can often fatten your Social Security benefits.

If you do own a home, consider making the most of your home equity. As this book is being written, mortgage rates are low. If you have not refinanced your home, do so now. With long-term mortgage rates below 5 percent in 2012, you can slash your monthly payments and put the savings to work in your investment portfolio. If you are retired and have considerable equity in your home, you might consider a "reverse mortgage," where you borrow against the value of your home. Instead of paying your mortgage off, you gradually receive payments up to the amount of the loan. Of course this is not saving, and it will not provide an inheritance for your heirs, but it may help you meet your expenses.

> Even if you failed to save enough on a regular schedule earlier in your life—the first fundamental rule for achieving financial security—it's never too late to start.

Live modestly and avoid taking on credit card debt. Even if you failed to save enough on a regular schedule earlier in your life—the first fundamental rule for achieving financial security—it's never too late to start.

II

INDEX

"Diz 'n' me gonna win 50 games."

"We will land a man on the moon and return him safely in this decade."

"I shall return."

Each of these major plans met one great test: clarity. If your plan is clear, it will be easier for you to stay on plan. The other test of a good plan is that it works. It works for you because it's doable. It works in the market because it's realistic. It works because it helps you achieve *your* objectives.

Great coaches all agree with a simple summary of how to succeed in athletics: Plan your play and play your plan. That's why you'll want to develop a clear and simple financial plan *and* stay the course.

Here, we present a remarkably simple plan for investing that uses low-cost index funds as your primary investment vehicles. Index funds simply buy and hold the stocks (or bonds) in all or part of the market. By buying a share in a "total market" index fund, you acquire an ownership share in all the major businesses in the economy. Index funds eliminate the anxiety and expense of trying to predict which individual stocks, bonds, or mutual funds will beat the market.

This simple investment strategy—indexing— has outperformed all but a handful of the thousands of equity and bond funds that are sold to the public.

This simple investment strategy—indexing—has outperformed all but a handful of the thousands of equity and bond funds that are sold to the public. But you wouldn't know this when Wall Street throws everything but the kitchen sink at you to convince you otherwise. This is the plan we use ourselves for our retirement funds, and this is the plan we urge you to follow, too.

NOBODY KNOWS MORE THAN THE MARKET

It is difficult for most investors to believe that the stock market is actually smarter or better informed than they are. Most financial professionals still do not accept the premise—perhaps because they earn lucrative fees and believe they can pick and choose the best stocks and beat the market. (As the author Upton Sinclair observed a century ago, "It is difficult to get a man to understand something when his salary depends upon his not understanding it.") The cold truth is that our financial markets, while prone to occasional excesses of either optimism or pessimism, are actually smarter than almost all individuals. Almost no investor consistently outperforms the market either by predicting its movements or by selecting particular stocks.

Why is it that you can't hear some favorable piece of news on the radio or TV or read it on the Internet and use that information to make a favorable trade? Because

The Elements of Investing

an army of profit-seeking, full-time professionals will have likely already pounced on the news to drive the stock price up before you have a chance to act. That's why the most important pieces of news (such as takeover offers) are announced when the market is closed. By the time trading opens the next day, prices already reflect the offer. You can be sure that whatever news you hear has already been reflected in stock prices. Something that everyone knows is not worth knowing. Jason Zweig, the personal finance columnist for the *Wall Street Journal*, describes the situation as follows:

> *I'm often accused of "disempowering" people because I refuse to give any credence to anyone's hope of beating the market. The knowledge that I don't need to know anything is an incredibly profound form of knowledge. Personally, I think it's the ultimate form of empowerment. . . . If you can plug your ears to every attempt (by anyone) to predict what the markets will do, you will outperform nearly every other investor alive over the long run. Only the mantra of "I don't know, and I don't care" will get you there.*

*Jason Zweig, *Your Money and Your Brain* (New York: Simon & Schuster, 2007).

This doesn't mean that the overall market is always correctly priced. Stock markets often make major mistakes, and market prices tend to be far more volatile than the underlying conditions warrant. Internet and technology stocks got bid up to outlandish prices in early 2000, and some tech stocks subsequently declined by 90 percent or more. Housing prices advanced to bubble levels during the early 2000s. When the bubble popped in 2008 and 2009, it not only brought house prices down, it also destroyed the stocks of banks and other financial institutions around the world.

> Nobody knows more than the market.

But don't for a minute think that professional financial advice would have saved you from the financial tsunami. Professionally managed funds also loaded up with Internet and bank stocks—even at the height of their respective bubbles—because that's where the action was and managers wanted to "participate" (and not get left out). And professionally managed funds tend to have their lowest cash positions at market tops and highest cash positions at market bottoms. Only after the fact do we all have 20–20 vision that the past mispricing was "obvious." As the legendary investor Bernard Baruch once noted, "Only liars manage always to be out of the market during bad times and in during good times."

Rex Sinquefield of Dimensional Fund Advisors puts it in a particularly brutal way: "There are three classes of people who do not believe that markets work: the Cubans, the North Koreans, and active managers."

THE INDEX FUND SOLUTION

We have believed for many years that investors will be much better off bowing to the wisdom of the market and investing in low-cost, broad-based index funds, which simply buy and hold all the stocks in the market as a whole. As more and more evidence accumulates, we have become more convinced than ever of the effectiveness of index funds. Over 10-year periods, broad stock market index funds have regularly outperformed two-thirds or more of the actively managed mutual funds.

And the amount by which index funds trounce the typical mutual fund manager is staggeringly large. The following table compares the performance of active managers of broadly diversified mutual funds with the Standard & Poor's (S&P) 500 stock index of the largest corporations in the

United States. Each decade about three-quarters of the active managers must hang their heads in shame for being beaten by the popular stock market index.

Percentage of Actively Managed Mutual Funds Outperformed by the S&P 500 Index (Periods through June 30, 2012)

1 Year	3 Years	5 Years	10 Years	20 Years
93%	83%	81%	77%	73%

Sources: Lipper and The Vanguard Group.

The superiority of indexing as an investment strategy is further demonstrated by comparing the percentage returns earned by the typical actively managed mutual fund with a mutual fund that simply invests in all 500 stocks included in the S&P 500 stock index. The table on the following page shows that the index fund beats the average active fund by more than a full percentage point per year, year after year.*

---

*We show these comparisons versus the S&P 500 index because "total stock market" funds (the ones we recommend) have only recently come into existence.

Average Annual Returns of Actively Managed Mutual Funds Compared with S&P 500
20 years, Ending June 30, 2012

S&P 500 Index Fund	8.34%
Average Active Equity Mutual Fund[a]	7.00%
Shortfall	+1.34%

[a]Consists of all Lipper equity mutual fund categories.
Sources: Lipper, Wilshire, and The Vanguard Group.

Why does this happen? Are the highly paid professional managers incompetent? No, they certainly are not.

Here's why investors as a total group cannot earn more than the market return. All the stocks that are outstanding need to be held by someone. Professional investors as a whole are responsible for about 90 percent of all stock market trading. While the ultimate holders may be individuals through their pension plans, 401(k) plans, or IRAs, professional managers, as a group, cannot beat the market because they *are* the market.

Because the players in the market must, on average, earn the market return and winners' winnings will equal losers' losses, investing is called a *zero-sum game*. If some investors are fortunate enough to own only the stocks that have done better than the overall market, then it must follow that some other investors must be holding the stocks that have done worse. We can't and don't live in Garrison Keillor's mythical Lake Wobegon, where everybody is above average.

But why do professionals as a group do *worse* than the market? In fact, they do earn the market return—*before expenses*. The average actively managed mutual fund charges about one percentage point of assets each year for managing the portfolio. It is the expenses charged by professional "active" managers that drag their return well below that of the market as a whole.

Low-cost index funds charge only one-tenth as much for portfolio management. Index funds do not need to hire highly paid security analysts to travel around the world in a vain attempt to find "undervalued" securities. In addition, actively managed funds tend to turn over their portfolios about once a year. This trading incurs the costs of brokerage commissions, spreads between bid and asked prices, and "market impact costs" (the effect of big buy or sell orders on prices). Professional managers underperform the market as a whole by the amount of their management expenses and transaction costs.

Those costs go into the pockets of the croupiers of the financial system, not into your retirement funds. That's why active managers do not beat the market—and why the market beats them.

DON'T *SOME* BEAT THE MARKET?

Don't *some* managers beat the market? We often read about those rare investment managers who have managed to beat the market over the last quarter, or the last year, or even the last several years. Sure, some managers do beat the market—but that's not the real question. The real question is this: Will you, or anyone else, be able to pick the managers who *will* beat the market in advance?

That's a really tough one. Here's why:

1. Only a few managers beat the market. Since 1970, you can count on the fingers of one hand the number of managers who have managed to beat the market by any meaningful amount. And chances are that as more and more ambitious, skillful, hard-working managers with fabulous computer capabilities join the competition for "performance," it will continue to get harder

and harder for any one professional to do better than the other pros who now do 95 percent of the daily trading.

2. Nobody—repeat, nobody—has been able to figure out in advance which funds will do better. The failure to forecast certainly includes all the popular public rating sources, including Morningstar.

3. Funds that beat the market "win" by less than those that got beaten by the market "lose." This means that fund buyers' "slugging percentage" is even lower than the already discouraging win-loss ratio.

The only forecast based on past performance that works is the forecast of which funds will do *badly*. Funds that have done really poorly in the past do tend to perform poorly in the future. Talk about small consolation! And the reason for this persistence is that it is typically the very high-cost funds that show the poorest relative performance, and—unlike stock picking ability—those high investment fees do persist year after year.

The financial media are quick to celebrate managers who have recently beaten the market as investment geniuses. These investment managers appear on TV opining confidently about the direction of the market and about which stocks are particularly attractive for purchase. Should we then place our bets on the stock jockeys who have recently been on a hot streak? No, because there is no long-term persistence to above-average performance. Just because a manager beat the market *last* year does not mean he or she is likely to continue to do so again *next* year. The probability of continuing a winning streak is no greater than the probability of flipping heads in the next fair toss of a coin, even if you have flipped several heads in a row in your previous tosses. The top-rated funds in any decade bear no resemblance to the top-rated funds in the next decade. Mutual fund "performance" is almost as random as the market.

The *Wall Street Journal* provided an excellent example in January 2009 of how ephemeral "superior" investment performance can be. During the nine-year period through December 31, 2007, 14 equity mutual funds had managed to beat the S&P 500 for nine years in a row. Those funds were advertised to the public as the best vehicles for individual investors. How many of those funds do you think

2008 Return (%)

Return	Fund
−35	M&N Pro Blend
−37	S&P 500
−40	Amer Funds Fundamental
−40	Target Growth
−41	Lord Abbett Alpha
−42	T. Rowe Price Growth
−43	JP Morgan Small Cap
−46	Hartford Cap Appreciation
−47	AIM Capital Development
−50	Columbia Acorn Select
−49	T. Rowe Price New Era
−52	Fidelity Select Natural Resources
−53	Jennision Natural Resources
−54	Fidelity Adv Energy
−61	Ivy Global Natural Resources

And Then There Was One
Source: Wall Street Journal, January 5, 2009. Reprinted with permission of the *Wall Street Journal,* copyright © 2009 Dow Jones & Company, Inc. All Rights Reserved Worldwide. License number 2257121352481.

managed to beat the market in 2008? As the figure above shows, there was only one out of 14. Study after study comes to the same conclusion. Chasing hot performance is a costly and self-defeating exercise. Don't do it!

Are there any exceptions to the rule? Of all the professional money managers, Warren Buffett's record stands out as the most extraordinary. For over 40 years, Buffett's company, Berkshire Hathaway, has earned a rate of return for his stockholders twice as large as the stock market as a whole. But that record was not achieved only by his ability to purchase "undervalued" stocks, as it is often portrayed in the press. Buffett buys companies and holds them. (He has suggested that the correct holding period for a stock is forever.) *And* he has taken an active role in the management of the companies in which he has invested, such as the Washington Post, one of his earliest successes. And he uses the 'float' from insurance operations to get low-cost financial leverage. Even Buffett has suggested that most people would be far better off simply investing in index funds. So has David Swensen, the brilliant portfolio manager for the Yale University endowment fund.

We are convinced there will be "another Warren Buffett" over the next 40 years. There may even be several of them. But we are even more convinced we will never know in advance who they will be. As the previous figure makes clear, past performance is an unreliable guide to the future. Finding the next Warren Buffett is like looking for a needle in a haystack. We recommend that you buy the haystack instead, in the form of a low-cost index fund.

INDEX BONDS

If indexing has advantages in the stock market, its superiority is even greater in the bond market. You would *never* want to hold just one bond (such as an IOU from General Motors or Chrysler) in your portfolio—any single bond issuer could get into financial deficiency and be unable to repay you in full. That's why you need a broadly diversified portfolio of bonds—making a mutual fund essential. And it's wise to use bond index funds: They have regularly proved superior to actively managed bond funds. The table shows that the vast majority of actively managed bond funds have been beaten by bond index funds, particularly in the short-term and intermediate maturities.

Percentage of Actively Managed Bond Funds Outperformed by Government- and Corporate-Bond Indexes (10 years through June 30, 2012)

	Government	Corporate
Short-term	100%	94%
Intermediate term	100%	97%
Long-term	80%	91%

Sources: Morningstar, Barclays Capital, and The Vanguard Group.

INDEX INTERNATIONALLY

Indexing has also proved its merits in non-U.S. markets. Most global equity managers have been outperformed by a low-cost index fund that buys all the stocks in the MSCI EAFE (Europe, Australasia, and Far East) index of non-U.S. stocks in developed markets. Even in the less efficient emerging markets, index funds regularly outperform active managers. The very inefficiency of the trading markets in many emerging markets (lack of liquidity, large bid-ask spreads, high transaction costs) makes a high-turnover, active management investment strategy inadvisable. Indexing has even worked well in markets such as China, where there have apparently been many past instances of market manipulation.

INDEX FUNDS HAVE BIG ADVANTAGES

A major advantage of indexing is that index funds are tax efficient. Actively managed funds can create large tax liabilities if you hold them outside your tax-advantaged retirement plans. To the extent that your funds generate capital gains from their portfolio turnover, this active trading creates taxable income for you. And short-term capital gains are taxed at ordinary income tax rates that can go well over 50 percent when state income taxes are considered. Index funds, in contrast, are long-term buy-and-hold investors and typically do not generate significant capital gains or taxable income. To overcome the drag of expenses and taxes, an actively managed fund would have to outperform the market by 4.3 percentage points per year just to break even with index funds.* The odds that you can find an actively managed mutual fund that will perform that much better than an index fund are virtually zero.

Let's summarize the advantages of index funds. First, they simplify investing. You don't need to evaluate the thousands of actively managed funds and somehow pick the best. Second, index funds are cost efficient and tax efficient. (Active managers' trading in and out of securities can be costly and will tend to increase your capital gains tax liability.) Finally, they are predictable. While you are sure to lose money when the market declines, you won't end up doing far more poorly than the market, as many investors did when their mutual fund managers loaded up with Internet stocks in early

---

*Estimated by Mark Kritzman, CEO, Windham Capital Management.

2000 or with bank stocks in 2008. Investing in index funds won't permit you to boast at the golf club or at the beauty parlor that you were able to buy an individual stock or fund that soared. That's why critics like to call indexing "guaranteed mediocrity." But we liken it to playing a winner's game where you are virtually guaranteed to do better than average, because your return will not have been dragged down by high investment costs.

ONE WARNING

Not all index funds are created equal, however. Beware: Some index funds charge unconscionably high management fees. We believe you should buy only those domestic common-stock funds that charge one-fifth of 1 percent or less annually as management expenses. And while the fees for investing in international funds tend to be higher than for U.S. funds, we believe you should limit yourself to the lowest-cost international index funds as well. (We list our specific recommendations in a later chapter.)

You may also want to consider exchange-traded index funds, or ETFs. These are index funds that trade on the major stock exchanges and can be bought and sold like stocks. ETFs are available for broad U.S. and foreign indexes as well as for various market sectors. They have some advantages over mutual funds. They often have even lower expense ratios than index funds. They also allow an investor to buy and sell at any time during the day (rather than once a day at closing prices) and thus are favored by professional traders for hedging. Finally, they can be even more tax efficient than mutual funds since they can redeem shares without generating a taxable event.

ETFs are not suitable, however, for individuals making periodic payments into a retirement plan such as an IRA or 401(k) because each payment will incur a brokerage charge that could be a substantial percentage of small contributions. With no-load index funds, no transaction fees are levied on contributions. Moreover, mutual funds will automatically reinvest all dividends back into the fund whereas additional transactions could be required to reinvest ETF dividends. We recommend that individuals making periodic contributions to a retirement plan use low-cost indexed mutual funds rather than ETFs.

Let's wrap up this chapter on index funds with two more pieces of advice. The first concerns how an investor should choose among different types of broad-based index funds. The best-known of the broad stock market mutual funds and ETFs in the United States track the S&P 500 index of the largest stocks. We prefer using a broader index that includes more smaller-company stocks, such as the Russell 3000 index or the Dow-Wilshire 5000 index. Funds that track these broader indexes are often referred to as "total stock market" index funds. More than 80 years of stock market history confirm that portfolios of smaller stocks have produced a higher rate of return than the return of the S&P 500 large-company index. While smaller companies are undoubtedly less stable and riskier than large firms, they are likely—on average—to produce somewhat higher future returns. Total stock market index funds are the better way for investors to benefit from the long-run growth of economic activity.

We have one final piece of advice for those stock market junkies who feel that, despite all the evidence to the contrary, they really do know more than the market does. If you must try to beat the market by identifying the next Google or the next Warren Buffett, we are not about to insist that you not do it. Your odds of success are at least better in the stock market than at the racetrack or gambling casino, and investing in individual stocks can be a lot of fun. But we do advise you to keep your serious retirement money in index funds. Do what professional investors increasingly do: Index the core of your portfolio and then, if you must, make individual bets around the edges. But have the major core of your investment—and especially your retirement funds—in a well-diversified set of stock and bond index funds. You can then "play the market" with any extra funds you have with far less risk that you will undermine your chances for a comfortable and worry-free retirement.

CONFESSION

Nobody's perfect. We certainly aren't. For example, one of us has a major commitment to the stock of a single company—an unusual company called Berkshire Hathaway. He has owned it for 35 years and has no intention to sell. If that's bad enough, ponder this: He checks the price almost every day! Of course, it's nuts—and he knows it, but just can't help himself. Another example: The other author delights in buying individual stocks and has a significant commitment to China. He enjoys the game of trying to pick winners and believes "China" is a major story for his grandchildren. (*Please note*, in both cases, our retirement funds are safely indexed—and our children use index funds, too!)

III

DIVERSIFY

A very sad story illustrates the crucial need for investors to diversify their investment holdings. It concerns a secretary who worked for the Enron Corporation during its heyday in the late 1990s and early 2000s. Enron was one of the new-age companies that formed to revolutionize the market for electric power and mass communications. Two charismatic masterminds, Kenneth Lay and Jeff Skilling, ran Enron and were regularly lionized by the press for their skill and daring. Enron stock was the darling of Wall Street, and it seemed to defy gravity by rising steadily into the stratosphere.

Like most major companies, Enron had established a 401(k) retirement plan for its employees, offering a range of options for the regular savings contributions that would be automatically deducted in each pay period. One of the investment options in the plan was to put those contributions into Enron stock. The chief executive officer, Ken Lay, strongly recommended that employees use Enron stock as their preferred retirement vehicle. Enron was likened to Elvis Presley revolutionizing the music scene. The old power companies were like old fogies dancing to the music of Lawrence Welk. And so the secretary put all of her retirement savings into Enron stock, and how glad she was that she did. As the stock soared, while she had never earned more than a modest secretary's pay, her retirement kitty was worth almost $3 million. During the next year, she looked forward to retirement and a life of leisure and world travel.

Well, she got her wish for more "leisure." As we now know, Enron had been built on a mosaic of phony accounting and fraudulent trading schemes. Jeff Skilling went to jail, and Ken Lay died while awaiting trial. The stock price collapsed, and the secretary's entire retirement kitty vaporized. She lost not only her job, but also her life savings. She had made the mistake of putting all her investments in one basket. Not only did she fail to diversify her investments, but she put herself in double jeopardy because she took exactly the same risks with her portfolio as she did with her income from employment. She failed to heed one of the few absolute rules of investing: Diversify, Diversify, Diversify.

James Rhodes spent his entire career in the automobile industry casting iron dies that turned sheet metal into fenders, hoods, and roofs. When he left the business, he and his wife decided that they could securely invest their entire accumulated savings in Chrysler bonds, paying an attractive 8 percent interest rate per year. They, like so many autoworkers, had faith in the iconic big three automakers' ability to survive even in the worst economic times. And the generous interest payments allowed them to continue to enjoy a comfortable middle-class lifestyle—for a while. Now the Rhodeses' faith in the auto industry and their retirement savings have evaporated. Many individual investors lost almost everything as the bankruptcy of Chrysler and General Motors left the secured bondholders with no continuing interest payments and only a minimal equity stake in the bankrupt companies.

These very sad stories make all too clear the cardinal rule of investing: Broad diversification is essential.

Enron, Chrysler, and General Motors are not isolated examples. Surprisingly, many large and seemingly stable industrial companies have gone belly up. Even large financial institutions—banks such as Wachovia, investment firms such as Lehman Brothers, insurance companies such as AIG—have gone bankrupt or were forced into mergers or government trusteeship after the value of their stocks cratered. And many financial executives, who should have known better, were wiped out because they had all of their assets invested in the firms where they worked, feeling loyalty and confidence in "their" company. If we had our way, no employee contributions to a 401(k) plan could be invested in their own company. Protect yourself: Every investor should always diversify.

> Protect yourself: Every investor
> should always diversify.

DIVERSIFY ACROSS ASSET CLASSES

What does diversification mean in practice? It means that when you invest in the stock market, you want a broadly diversified portfolio holding hundreds of stocks. For people of modest means, and even quite wealthy people, the way to accomplish that is to buy one or more low-cost equity index mutual funds. The fund pools the money from thousands of investors and buys a portfolio of hundreds of individual common stocks. The mutual fund collects all the dividends, does all the accounting, and lets mutual fund owners reinvest all cash distributions in more shares of the fund if they so wish.

While some mutual funds are specialized, concentrating in a particular market segment such as biotechnology companies or Chinese companies, we recommend that the fund you choose have a mandate of broad diversification and hold securities in a wide spectrum of companies spanning all the major industries. We will give you tips in Chapter 5 on how to select the best, lowest-cost, and most diversified investment funds available.

Diversify across securities, across asset classes, across markets—and across time.

By holding a wide variety of company stocks, the investor tends to reduce risk because most economic events do not affect all companies the same way. A favorable event such as the approval of a new pharmaceutical could be a major boost for the company that discovered the drug. At the same time, it could be damaging to companies making older competing products. Even deep recessions will have different effects on companies catering to different demographic groups. As people tightened their belts, they buy less from Tiffany's and more from Wal-Mart.

Just as you need to diversify by holding a large number of individual stocks in different industries to moderate your investment risk, so you also need to diversify by holding different asset classes. One asset class that belongs in most portfolios is bonds. Bonds are basically IOUs issued by corporations and government units. (The government units might be foreign, state and local, or government-sponsored enterprises such as the Federal National Mortgage Association, popularly known as Fannie Mae.) And just as you should diversify by holding a broadly diversified stock fund, so should you hold a broadly diversified bond fund.

The U.S. Treasury issues large amounts of bonds. These issues are considered the safest of all and these bonds are the one type of security where diversification is not essential. Unlike common stocks, whose dividends and earnings fluctuate with the ups and downs of the company's business, bonds pay a fixed dollar amount of interest.

If the U.S. Treasury offers a $1,000 20-year, 5 percent bond, that bond will pay $50 per year until it matures, when the principal will be repaid. Corporate bonds are less safe, but widely diversified bond portfolios have provided reasonably stable interest returns over time.

High-quality bonds can moderate the risk of a common stock portfolio by providing offsetting variations to the inevitable ups and downs of the stock market. For example, in 2008, common stock prices fell in both U.S. and foreign markets as investors correctly anticipated a severe worldwide recession. But a U.S. Treasury bond portfolio rose in price as the monetary authorities lowered interest rates to stimulate the economy. If you are confused about how bond prices change as interest rates rise and fall, just remember the "see-saw" rule: When interest rates fall, bond prices rise. When interest rates rise, bond prices fall.

Other asset classes can reduce risk as well. In 2008, all stock markets around the world fell together. There was no place to hide. But during most years, while some national markets zig, others zag. For example, during 2009, when all the major industrial countries were sinking into a deep recession, countries such as China, which was developing its vast central and western regions, continued to grow.

During inflationary periods, real estate and real assets such as timber and oil have usually provided better inflation hedges than ordinary industrial companies whose profit margins are likely to get squeezed when raw material prices rise. Hence, real estate and commodities have proven to be useful diversifiers in many periods. Gold and gold-mining companies have often had a unique role as the commodity of choice for diversification. Gold has historically been the asset to which investors have fled during uncertain and perilous times. It is often called the hedge against Armageddon.

If you purchase the very broad-based index funds we list later in this book, you will achieve some of the benefits of direct real estate and commodities investing. So-called "total stock market" funds will include both real estate companies and commodity products. Broad equity diversification can be achieved with one-stop shopping.

DIVERSIFY ACROSS MARKETS

The stocks of companies in foreign markets such as Europe and Asia also can provide diversification benefits. To be sure, there is some truth to the expression that when the United States catches a cold, the rest of the developed world catches pneumonia; the market meltdowns and painful recessions of 2008–2009 were worldwide. But that does not mean that economic activity and stock markets in different developed nations always move in lockstep. During the 1990s, when the U.S. economy was booming, Japan's economy stagnated for the entire decade. During periods in the 2000s when the U.S. dollar was falling, the euro was rising, giving an added boost to European stocks. And even though globalization has linked our economies more and more closely, there is still good reason not to restrict your holding to U.S. stocks. To the extent that you hold automobile stocks in your portfolio, you should not limit yourself to Detroit. You are likely to be better off including Toyota and Honda in a diversified portfolio.

Does achieving extremely broad diversification seem completely out of reach for ordinary investors? Fear not. There are broadly invested, very low-cost funds that can provide one-stop shopping solutions. We will recommend a broadly diversified United States total stock market index fund that includes real estate companies and commodity producers, including gold miners. We will also show you how a non-U.S. total stock market fund can give you exposure to the entire world economy, including the fast-growing emerging markets. Similarly, a total bond market fund will provide you with a fully diversified bond portfolio. If you will follow the diversification principle here, we will show you, in Chapter 5, the specific funds that will allow you to put together a well-diversified portfolio at low cost.

DIVERSIFY OVER TIME

There is one final diversification lesson that we need to stress. *You should diversify over time.* Don't make all your investments at a single time. If you did, you might be unlucky enough to have put all of your money into the stock market during a market peak in early 2000. An investor who put everything in the market at the start of 2000 would have experienced a negative return over the entire decade. The 1970s were just as bad. And an investor who put everything in at the 1929 peak, like the father of one of the authors, would not have broken even for more than 20 years.

You can reduce risk by building up your investments slowly with regular, periodic investments over time. Investing regular amounts monthly or quarterly will ensure that you put some of your money to work during favorable periods, when prices are relatively low.

Investment advisers call this technique "dollar-cost averaging." With equal dollar investments over time, the investor buys fewer shares when prices are high and more shares when prices are low. It won't eliminate risk but it will ensure that you don't buy your entire portfolio at temporarily inflated prices. The experience of putting your entire investment in the stock market at a wrong time could sour you on common stocks for an entire lifetime, sadly compounding the problem.

With dollar-cost averaging, investors can actually come out better in a market where prices are volatile and end up exactly where they started than in a market where prices rise steadily year after year. Suppose that all investments are made in a broad stock market index fund and that $1,000 is invested each year over a five-year period. Now let's consider two scenarios: In the first scenario, the stock market is very volatile, declining sharply after the program is commenced and ending exactly where it started. In the second scenario, the stock market rises each year after the program begins. Before we look at the numbers, ask yourself under which scenario the investor is likely to do better. We bet that almost everybody would expect to have better investment results in the situation when the market goes straight up. Now let's look at the numbers.

The table on page 63 assumes that $1,000 is invested each year. In scenario one, the market falls immediately after the investment program begins; then it rises sharply and finally falls again, ending, in year five, exactly where it began. In scenario two, the market rises continuously and ends up 40 percent higher at the end of the period. While a total of exactly $5,000 is invested in both cases, the investor in the volatile market ends up with $6,048—a nice return of $1,048—even though the stock market ended exactly where it started. In the scenario where the market rose each year and ended up 40 percent from where it began, the investor's final stake is only $5,915.

Warren Buffett presents a lucid rationale for the investment principle illustrated above. In one of his published essays he says:

> *A short quiz: If you plan to eat hamburgers throughout your life and are not a cattle producer, should you wish for higher or lower prices for beef? Likewise, if you are going to buy a car from time to time but are not an auto manufacturer, should you prefer higher or lower car prices? These questions, of course, answer themselves.*

Dollar-Cost Averaging

Year	Volatile Flat Market			Rising Market		
	Amount Invested	Price of Index Fund	Number of Shares Purchased	Amount Invested	Price of Index Fund	Number of Shares Purchased
1	$1,000	$100	10	$1,000	$100	10
2	$1,000	$60	16.67	$1,000	$110	9.09
3	$1,000	$60	16.67	$1,000	$120	8.33
4	$1,000	$140	7.14	$1,000	$130	7.69
5	$1,000	$100	10	$1,000	$140	7.14
Amount invested	$5,000			$5,000		
Total shares purchased			60.48			42.25
Average cost of shares purchased	$82.67	($5,000/60.48)		$118.34	($5,000/42.25)	
Value at end	$6,048	(60.48 × $100)		$5,915	(42.25 × $140)	

But now for the final exam: If you expect to be a net saver during the next five years, should you hope for a higher or lower stock market during that period? Many investors get this one wrong. Even though they are going to be net buyers of stocks for many years to come, they are elated when stock prices rise and depressed when they fall. In effect, they rejoice because prices have risen for the "hamburgers" they will soon be buying. This reaction makes no sense. Only those who will be sellers of equities in the near future should be happy at seeing stocks rise. Prospective purchasers should much prefer sinking prices.

Dollar-cost averaging is not a panacea that eliminates the risk of investing in common stocks. It will not save your 401(k) plan from a devastating fall in value during a year such as 2008, because no plan can protect you from a punishing bear market. And you must have both the cash and the confidence to continue making the periodic investments even when the sky is the darkest. No matter how scary the financial news, no matter how difficult it is to see any signs of optimism, you must not interrupt the automatic-pilot nature of the program. Because if you do, you will lose the benefit of buying at least some of your shares after a sharp market decline when they are for sale at low-end prices. Dollar-cost averaging will give you this bargain: Your average price per share will be lower than the average price at which you bought shares. Why? Because you'll buy more shares at low prices and fewer at high prices.

Some investment advisors are not fans of dollar-cost averaging because the strategy is not optimal if the market does go straight up. (You would have been better off putting all $5,000 into the market at the beginning of the period.) But it does provide a reasonable insurance policy against poor future stock markets. And it does minimize the regret that inevitably follows if you were unlucky enough to have put all your money into the stock market during a peak period such as March of 2000 or October of 2007.

REBALANCE

Rebalancing is the technique used by professional investors to ensure that a portfolio remains efficiently diversified. It is not complicated, and we believe that individual investors should rebalance their portfolios as well. Since market prices change over time, so will the share of your portfolio that is in stocks or bonds. Rebalancing simply involves periodically checking the allocation of the different types of investments in your portfolio and bringing them back to your desired percentages if they get out of line. Rebalancing reduces the volatility and riskiness of your investment portfolio and can often enhance your returns.

Suppose you have decided that the portfolio balance that is most appropriate for your age and your comfort level has 60 percent in stocks and 40 percent in bonds. As you add to your retirement accounts, you put 60 percent of the new money into a stock fund and the remainder into a bond fund.

Movements in the bond and stock markets will tend to shift your allocation over time. Small changes (plus or minus 10 percent) should probably be ignored. But what if the stock market doubles in a short period and bond values stay constant? All of a sudden you would find that three-quarters of your portfolio is now invested in stocks and only one-quarter is allocated to bonds. That would change the overall market risk of your portfolio away from the balance you chose as best for you. Or what if the stock market falls sharply and bonds rise in price, as was the experience of investors in 2008? What do you do then?

The correct response is to make corrective changes in the mix of your portfolio. This is what we mean by "rebalancing." It involves not letting the asset proportions in your portfolio stray too far from the ideal mix you have chosen as best for you. Suppose the equity portion of your portfolio is too high. You could direct all new allocations, as well as the dividends paid from your equity investments, into bond investments. (If the balance is severely out of whack, you can shift some of your money from the equity fund you hold into bond investments.) If the proportion of your investments in bonds has risen so that it exceeds your desired allocation, you can move money into equities.

The right response to a fall in the price of one asset class is never to panic and sell out. Rather, you need the long-term discipline and personal fortitude to buy *more*. Remember: The lower stock prices go, the better the bargains if you are truly a long-term investor. Sharp market declines may make rebalancing appear a frustrating "way to lose even more money." But in the long run, investors who rebalance their portfolios in a disciplined way are well rewarded.

When markets are very volatile, rebalancing can actually increase your rate of return and, at the same time, decrease your risk by reducing the volatility of your portfolio.

The decade from 1996 through 2005 provides an excellent example. Suppose an investor's chosen allocation is 60 percent in stocks and 40 percent in bonds. Let's use a broad-based U.S. total stock market index fund for the equity portion of the portfolio and a total bond market index fund for the bonds to illustrate the advantages of rebalancing. The table on page 69 shows how rebalancing was able to increase the investor's return while reducing risk, as measured by the quarterly volatility of return.

If an investor had simply bought such a 60/40 portfolio at the start of the period and held on for 10 years, she would have earned an average rate of return of 8.08 percent per year. But if each year she rebalanced the portfolio to preserve the 60/40 mix, the return would have increased to almost 8½ percent. Moreover, the quarterly results would have been more stable, allowing the investor to sleep better at night.

During the decade January 1996 through December 2005, an annually rebalanced portfolio provided lower volatility and higher return.

The Importance of Rebalancing

Portfolio:[a] 60% Total Stock Market 40% Total Bond Market	Average Annual Return	Risk (Volatility)[b]
Annually rebalanced	8.46%	9.28
Never rebalanced	8.08%	10.05

[a]Stocks represented by a Russell 3000® total stock market fund. Bonds represented by a Lehman U.S. aggregate total bond market fund.
[b]The variation of your portfolio's annual return as measured by the standard deviation of return.

Why did rebalancing work so well? Suppose the investor rebalanced once a year at the beginning of January. (Don't be trigger-happy: Rebalance once a year.) During January 2000, near the top of the Internet craze, the stock portion of the portfolio rose well above 60 percent, so some stocks were sold and the proceeds put into bonds that had been falling in price as interest rates rose. The investor did not know we were near a stock market peak (the actual peak was in March 2000). But she was able to lighten up on stocks when they were selling at very high prices. When the rebalancing was done in January 2003, the situation was different. Stocks had fallen sharply (the low of the market occurred in October 2002) and bonds had risen in price as interest rates were reduced by the Federal Reserve. So money was taken from the bond part of the portfolio and invested in equities at what turned out to be quite favorable prices.

Rebalancing will not always increase returns. But it will always reduce the riskiness of the portfolio and it will always ensure that your actual allocation stays consistent with the right allocation for your needs and temperament.

Rebalancing will not always increase returns. But it will always reduce the riskiness of the portfolio and it will always ensure that your actual allocation stays consistent with the right allocation for your needs and temperament.

Investors will also want to consider rebalancing to change their portfolio's asset mix as they age. For most people, a more and more conservative asset mix that has a deliberately reduced equity component will provide less stress as they approach and then enter retirement.

IV

AVOID BLUNDERS

You, far more than the market or the economy, are the most important factor in your long-term investment success.

We're both in our seventies. America's favorite investor, Warren Buffett, is in his early eighties. The main difference between his spectacular results and our good results is not the economy and not the market, but the man from Omaha. He is simply a better investor than just about any other investor in the world, amateur or professional. Brilliant, consistently rational, and blessed with a superb mind for business, he concentrates more time and effort on being a better investor and is more disciplined.

One of the major reasons for Buffett's success is that he has managed to avoid the major mistakes that have crushed so many portfolios. Let's look at two examples. In early 2000, many observers declared that Buffett had somehow lost his touch. His Berkshire Hathaway portfolio had underperformed the popular high-tech funds that enjoyed spectacular returns by loading up on stocks of technology companies and Internet start-ups. Buffett avoided all tech stocks. He told his investors that he refused to invest in any company whose business he did not fully understand—and he didn't claim to understand the complicated, fast-changing technology business—or where he could not figure out how the business model would sustain a growing stream of earnings. Some said he was passé, a fuddy-duddy. Buffett had the last laugh when Internet-related stocks came crashing back to earth.

In 2005 and 2006, Buffett largely avoided the popular complex mortgage-backed securities and the derivatives that found their way into many investment portfolios.

Again, his view was that they were too complex and opaque. He called them "financial weapons of mass destruction." When in 2007 they brought down many a financial institution (and ravaged our entire financial system), Berkshire Hathaway avoided the worst of the financial meltdown.

Avoiding serious trouble, particularly troubles that come from incurring unnecessary risks, is one of the great secrets to investment success. Investors all too often beat themselves by making serious—and completely unnecessary—investment mistakes. In this chapter, we highlight the common investment mistakes that can prevent you from realizing your goals.

> As in so many human endeavors, the secrets to success are patience, persistence, and minimizing mistakes.

As in so many human endeavors, the secrets to success are patience, persistence, and minimizing mistakes. In driving, it's having no serious accidents; in tennis, the key is getting the ball back; and in investing, it's indexing—to avoid the expenses and mistakes that do so much harm to so many investors.

OVERCONFIDENCE

In recent years, a group of behavioral psychologists and financial economists have created the important new field of behavioral finance. Their research shows that we are not always rational and that in investing, we are often our worst enemies. We tend to be overconfident, harbor illusions of control, and get stampeded by the crowd. To be forewarned is to be forearmed.

At our two favorite universities, Yale and Princeton, psychologists are fond of giving students questionnaires asking how they compare with their classmates in respect to different skills. For example, students are asked: "Are you a more skillful driver than your average classmate?" Invariably, the overwhelming majority answer that they are above-average drivers compared with their classmates. Even when asked about their athletic ability, where one would think it was more difficult to delude oneself, students generally think of themselves as above-average athletes, and they see themselves as above-average dancers, conservationists, friends, and so on.

And so it is with investing. If we do make a success-ful investment, we confuse luck with skill. It was easy in early 2000 to delude yourself that you were an investment genius when your Internet stock doubled and then doubled again. The first step in dealing with the pernicious effects of overconfidence is to recognize how pervasive it is. In amateur tennis, the player who steadily returns the ball, with no fancy shots, is usually the player who wins. Similarly, the buy-and-hold investor who prudently holds a diversified portfolio of low-cost index funds through thick and thin is the investor most likely to achieve her long-term investment goals.

Investors should avoid any urge to forecast the stock market. Forecasts, even forecasts by recognized "experts," are unlikely to be better than random guesses. "It will fluctuate," declared J. P. Morgan when asked about his expectation for the stock market. He was right. All other market forecasts—usually estimating the overall direction of the stock market—are historically about 50 percent right and 50 percent wrong. You wouldn't bet much money on a coin toss, so don't even think of acting on stock market forecasts.

Why? Forecasts of many "real economy" developments based on hard data are wonderfully useful. So are weather forecasts. Market forecasting is many times more difficult. Market forecasts have a poor record because the market is already the aggregate result of many, many well-informed investors making their best estimates and expressing their views with real money. Predicting the stock market is really predicting how other investors will change the estimates they are now making with all their best efforts. This means that, for a market forecaster to be right, the consensus of all others must be wrong *and* the forecaster must determine in which direction—up or down—the market will be moved by changes in the consensus of those same active investors.

Warning: As human beings, we like to be told what the future will bring. Soothsayers and astrologists have made forecasts throughout history. A panoply of genial myths have been part of the human experience for centuries—and we're all still human. Buildings don't have a 13th floor; we avoid walking under ladders, toss salt over our shoulders, and don't step on cracks in the sidewalk. "Que sera, sera" has charm as a tune, but it gives no real satisfaction.

The largest, longest study of experts' economic forecasts was performed by Philip Tetlock, a professor at the Haas Business School of the University of California–Berkeley. He studied 82,000 predictions over 25 years by 300 selected experts. Tetlock concludes that expert predictions barely beat random guesses. Ironically, the more famous the expert, the less accurate his or her predictions tended to be.

So, as an investor, what should you do about forecasts—forecasts of the stock market, forecasts of interest rates, forecasts of the economy? Answer: Nothing. You can save time, anxiety, and money by ignoring all market forecasts.

As an investor, what should you do about forecasts—forecasts of the stock market, forecasts of interest rates, forecasts of the economy? Answer: Nothing. You can save time, anxiety, and money by ignoring all market forecasts.

BEWARE OF MR. MARKET

As people, we feel safety in numbers. Investors tend to get more and more optimistic, and unknowingly take greater and greater risks, during bull markets and periods of euphoria. That is why speculative bubbles feed on themselves. But any investment that has become a widespread topic of conversation among friends or has been hyped by the media is very likely to be unsuccessful.

Throughout history, some of the worst investment mistakes have been made by people who have been swept up in a speculative bubble. Whether with tulip bulbs in Holland during the 1630s, real estate in Japan during the 1980s, or Internet stocks in the United States during the late 1990s, following the herd—believing "this time it's different"—has led people to make some of the worst investment mistakes. Just as contagious euphoria leads investors to take greater and greater risks, the same self-destructive behavior leads many investors to throw in the towel and sell out near the market's bottom when pessimism is rampant and seems most convincing.

One of the most important lessons you can learn about investing is to avoid following the herd and getting caught up in market-based overconfidence *or* discouragement. Beware of "Mr. Market."

First described by Benjamin Graham, the father of investment analysis, two mythical characters compete for our attention as investors.* One is Mr. Market and one is Mr. Value. Mr. Value invents, manufactures, and sells all

---

*Benjamin Graham (with Jason Zweig), *The Intelligent Investor* (New York: HarperBusiness, 2003).

the many goods and services we all need. Working hard at repetitive and often boring tasks, conscientious Mr. Value beavers away day and night making our complex economy perform millions of important functions day after day. He's seldom exciting, but we know we can count on him to do his best to meet our wants.

While Mr. Value does all the work, Mr. Market has all the fun. Mr. Market has two malicious objectives. The first is to trick investors into *selling* stocks or mutual funds at or near the market bottom. The second is to trick investors into *buying* stocks or mutual funds at or near the top. Mr. Market tries to trick us into changing our investments at the wrong time—and he's really good at it. Sometimes terrifying, sometimes gently charming, sometimes compellingly positive, sometimes compelling negative, but always engaging, this malicious, high-maintenance economic gigolo has only one objective: to cause you to *do something*. Make changes, buy or sell—anything will do if you'll just do something. And then do something else. The more you do, the merrier he will be.

Mr. Market is expensive and the cost of transactions is the small part of the total cost. The large part of the total cost comes from the mistakes he tricks us into making—buying high and selling low. Look at the crafty devil's record of success. Here's how he has been tricking investors as a whole. In the next figure we superimpose the flows of money going into equity mutual funds against the general level of market prices. The lesson is unmistakable. Money flows into the funds when prices are high. Investors pour money into equity mutual funds at exactly the wrong time.

More money went into equity mutual funds during the fourth quarter of 1999 and the first quarter of 2000—just at the top of the market—than ever before. And most of the money that went into the market was directed to the high technology and Internet funds—the stocks that turned out to be the most overpriced and then declined the most during the subsequent bear market. And more money went out of the market during the third quarter of 2002 than ever before, as mutual funds were redeemed or liquidated—just at the market trough. Note also that during the punishing bear market of 2007–2008, new record withdrawals were made by investors who threw in the towel and sold their mutual fund shares—at record lows—just before the first, and often best, part of a market recovery.

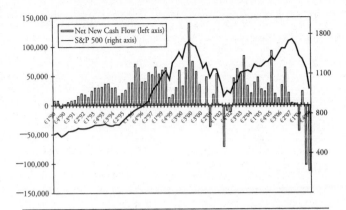

Cash Flow to Equity Funds Follows the Stock Market
Source: The Vanguard Group.

It's not today's price or even next year's price that matters; it's the price you'll get when it's your time to sell to provide spending money during your years of retirement. For most investors, retirement is a long way off in the future. Indeed, when pessimism is rampant and market prices are down is the worst time to sell out or to stop making regular investment contributions. The time to buy is when stocks are on sale.

Investing is like raising teenagers—"interesting" along the way as they grow into fine adults. Experienced parents know to focus on the long term, not the dramatic daily dust-ups. The same applies to investing. Don't let

Mr. Market trick you into either exuberance or distress. Just as you do when the weather is really extreme, remember the ancient counsel, "This too shall pass."

You don't care if it's cold and raining or warm and sunny 10,000 miles away because it's not *your* weather. The same detachment should apply to your 401(k) investments until you approach retirement. Even at age 60, chances are you will live another 25 years and your spouse may live several years more.

THE PENALTY OF TIMING

Does the timing penalty—the cost of second-guessing the market—make a big difference? You bet it does. The stock market as a whole has delivered an average rate of return of about 9½ percent over long periods of time. But that return only measures what a buy-and-hold investor would earn by putting money in at the start of the period and keeping her money invested through thick and thin. In fact, the returns actually earned by the average investor are at least two percentage points—almost one-fourth—lower because the money tends to come in at or near the top and out at or near the bottom.*

---

*Ilia D. Dichev, "What Are Stock Investors' Actual Historical Returns?" *American Economic Review* 97 (March 2007): 386–401.

In addition to the timing penalty, there is also a selection penalty. When money poured into equity mutual funds in late 1999 and early 2000, most of it went to the riskier funds—those invested in high tech and Internet stocks. The staid "value" funds, which held stocks selling at low multiples of earnings and with high dividend yields, experienced large withdrawals. During the bear market that followed, these same value funds held up very well while the "growth" funds suffered large price declines. That's why the gap between the actual returns of investors and the overall market returns is even larger than the two percentage point gap cited earlier.

Fortunately, there's hope. Mr. Market can only hurt us if we let him. That's why we all need to learn that getting tricked or duped by Mr. Market is actually *our* fault. As Mom said, we can only get teased or insulted or hurt by bad people if we let them. As an investor, you have one powerful way to keep from getting distressed by devilish Mr. Market: Ignore him. Just buy and hold one of the broad-based index funds that we list on pages 117–119.

MORE MISTAKES

Psychologists have identified a tendency in people to think they have control over events even when they have none. For investors, such an illusion can lead them to overvalue a losing stock in their portfolio. It also can lead people to imagine there are trends when none exist or believe they can spot a pattern in a stock price chart and thus predict the future. Charting is akin to astrology. The changes in stock prices are very close to a "random walk": There is no dependable way to predict the future movements of a stock's price from its past wanderings.

The same holds true for supposed "seasonal" patterns, even if they appear to have worked for decades in the past. Once everyone knows there is a Santa Claus rally in the stock market between Christmas and New Year's Day, the "pattern" will evaporate. This is because investors will buy one day before Christmas and sell one day before the end of the year to profit from the supposed regularity. But then investors will have to jump the gun even earlier, buying two days before Christmas and selling two days before the end of the year. Soon all the buying will be done well before Christmas and the selling will take place right around Christmas. Any apparent stock market "pattern" that can be discovered will not last—as long as there are people around who will try to exploit it.

Psychologists also remind us that investors are far more distressed by losses than they are delighted by gains. This leads people to discard their winners if they need cash and hold onto their losers because they don't want to recognize or admit that they made a mistake. Remember: Selling winners means paying capital gains taxes while selling losers can produce tax deductions. So if you need to sell, sell your losers. At least that way you get a tax deduction rather than an increase in your tax liability.

MINIMIZE COSTS

There is one investment truism that, if followed, can dependably increase your investment returns: Minimize your investment costs. We have spent two lifetimes thinking about which mutual fund managers will have the best performance year in and year out. Here's what we now know: It was and is hopeless.

> There is one investment truism that, if followed, can dependably increase your investment returns: Minimize your investment costs.

Here's why: Past performance is *not* a good predictor of future returns. What *does* predict investment performance are the fees charged by the investment manager. The higher the fees you pay for investment advice, the lower your investment return. As our friend Jack Bogle likes to say: In the investment business, "You get what you *don't* pay for."

Let's demonstrate this proposition with the simple table shown on page 89. We look at all equity mutual funds over a 10-year period and measure the rate of return produced for their investors as well as all the costs charged and the implicit costs of portfolio turnover—the cost of buying and selling portfolio holdings. We then divide the funds into quartiles and show the average returns and average costs for each quartile. The lowest-cost quartile funds produce the best returns.

If you want to own a mutual fund with top quartile performance, buy a fund with low costs. Of course, the quintessential low-cost funds are the index funds we recommend throughout this book. If we measure *after-tax* returns, recognizing that high turnover funds tend to be tax inefficient, our conclusion holds with even greater force.

Costs and Net Returns: All General Equity Funds

	12/31/2002–12/31/2011 Annual Total Return	Latest Total Expense Ratio	Annual Portfolio Turnover
Low-cost quartile	5.97%	0.64%	51.4%
Quartile two	5.95%	1.08%	68.9%
Quartile three	5.76%	1.42%	70.6%
High-cost quartile	5.06%	2.09%	84.3%

Sources: Lipper and Bogle Financial Research Center.

While we are on the subject of minimizing costs, we need to warn you to beware of stockbrokers. Brokers have one priority: to make a good income for themselves. That's why they do what they do the way they do it. The stockbroker's real job is not to make money *for* you but to make money *from* you. Of course, brokers tend to be nice, friendly, and personally enjoyable for one major reason: Being friendly enables them to get more business. So don't get confused. Your broker is your broker—period.

The typical broker "talks to" about 75 customers who collectively invest about $40 million. (Think for a moment about how many friends you have and how much time it takes you to develop each of those friendships.) Depending on the deal he has with his firm, your broker gets about 40 percent of the commissions you pay. So if he wants a $100,000 income, he needs to gross $250,000 in commissions charged to customers. Now do the math. If he needs to make $200,000, he'll need to gross $500,000. That means he needs to take that money from you and each of his other customers. Your money goes from your pocket to his pocket. That's why being "friends" with a stockbroker can be so expensive. Like Mr. Market, a broker has one priority: Getting you to take action, *any* action.

We urge you not to engage in "gin rummy" behavior. Don't jump from stock to stock or from mutual fund to fund as if you were selecting and discarding cards in a gin rummy game and thereby running up your commission costs (and probably adding to your tax bill as well). In fact, we don't think individual investors should try to buy individual stocks or try to pick particular actively managed mutual funds. Buy and hold a low-cost, broad-based index fund and you are likely to enjoy well-above-average returns because of the low costs you pay.

V

KEEP IT SIMPLE

In his attempts to unlock the complex secrets of the universe, Albert Einstein, the greatest scientist of the twentieth century, had one overriding maxim: "Everything should be made as simple as possible—but no simpler." We agree.

We know that the financial press is full of stories about the complexity of modern finance and that the investment world often appears frighteningly complex. But despite all the convoluted gimmicks some charlatans would like to sell you (because they are so profitable for the sellers), you can prosper by embracing simplicity.

That's why this chapter presents some very simple, easy-to-understand and easy-to-follow rules to help you achieve financial security. While some individuals have uniquely complex financial circumstances, we believe the rules we offer will work well for almost all investors. And the portfolio we will present "gets it right" for at least 90 percent of individual investors. We leave out—on purpose—all sorts of complicated details that really are just minor adjustments for the unusual circumstances that might affect particular individuals.*

In this section, we first review the simple rules for successful long-term investing. We then present, for you and the loved one we hope you'll discuss it with, the KISS (Keep It Simple, *Sweetheart*) portfolio. We think our rules and portfolio recommendations contain the very best advice that all investors require.

---

*If your financial or tax situation *is* especially complex, then seek the advice of a tax attorney or financial adviser. You will be better off with a "fee only" adviser. Advisers who earn commissions from selling you specialized investments are more likely to recommend high-expense financial products from which they can earn substantial commissions.

The KISS portfolio "gets it right" for at least 90 percent of individual investors.

REVIEW OF BASIC RULES

Here are the basic rules in abbreviated form. We have discussed most of them in earlier chapters.

1. *Save early and regularly.*

   The most important step you can take to building a comfortable nest egg and providing for a worry-free retirement is to start saving early and to keep saving regularly. There is no simple road to riches for you and your family. The secret to getting wealthy is that there is no secret. The only way to get rich—unless you inherit or marry a fortune or hit the lottery—is to get rich slowly. Start early and contribute as much as possible to your savings for as long as possible.

2. *Use the help of your employer and Uncle Sam to supercharge your savings.*

   We are amazed and distressed at how many people do not take full advantage of their employer's 401(k) or 403(b) retirement security plan. Sadly, many people do not even join the plan, even when their employer would match every dollar the employee saves. And Uncle Sam contributes a lot, too, because your contributions are not taxed until many years later, when you withdraw money needed to enjoy your retirement.

3. *Set aside a cash reserve.*

As the bumper sticker tells us, stuff happens. We need cash reserves for those "cost surprises" that we learn to expect as part of life. Such reserves should be invested in high-quality, short-term instruments because safety of principal and assured liquidity are your paramount concerns. The size of the cash reserve is up to you, but most financial planners suggest that in retirement, when no longer earning cash income, you set aside at least six months of living expenses. While you should not take on a lot of risk by stretching for higher returns, you should minimize costs as is appropriate with all financial instruments. The one investment lesson we are absolutely sure of is that the higher the expenses you pay the provider of any investment service, the lower will be the return to you.

The cash reserve could be invested in government-guaranteed bank deposits or in safe money-market funds. Shop for the highest rate available. Internet banks often offer the best rates. You may use savings accounts or bank certificates of deposit (CDs), but make sure that any savings deposit or CD is put in a bank that is insured by the Federal Deposit Insurance Corporation (FDIC).

While the money-market funds listed later are not insured, they often have higher rates and they give you the advantage of free checking (for bills of $250 or more). These money-market funds typically buy very large CDs from banks or they purchase the short-term obligations of prime corporate borrowers. If you want to be super safe, you can buy the money funds listed on page 99 that invest only in obligations guaranteed by the U.S. government. (These are called "government" or "Treasury" money-market funds.)

The lists in the table on the following page also include tax-exempt money-market funds. These funds invest in obligations of state and local governments, and the interest paid by these funds is exempt from federal taxation. You might also check whether state tax-exempt money-market funds exist for your state of residence. These funds can avoid state income taxes as well as federal taxes.

4. *Make sure you are covered by insurance.*

   If you are the breadwinner in your family and your spouse and children are dependent on you for support, you need life insurance and long-term disability insurance. And you need medical insurance. But when you buy insurance, remember the KISS principle: Buy simple, low-cost term life insurance, not complex "whole life" insurance, which combines a high-cost investment program with the life insurance you need.

   The main cost driver of disability insurance is the coverage for lost income when you can't work for a few months. You may decide to self-insure against this moderate risk to reduce your

Selected Low-Cost Money-Market Funds

Fund Name	Ticker Symbol	Expense Ratio	Five-Year Rate of Return[a]
Vanguard Prime Money Market www.vanguard.com; 800-662-7447	VMMXX	0.20%	0.84%
Vanguard Admiral Treasury Money Market Fund www.vanguard.com; 800-662-7447	VUSXX	0.12%	0.61%
Vanguard Tax-Exempt Money Market www.vanguard.com; 800-662-7447	VMSXX	0.17%	0.69%
Fidelity Cash Reserves www.fidelity.com; 800-343-3548	FDRXX	0.37%	0.87%
Fidelity Government Money Market Fund www.fidelity.com; 800-343-3548	SPAXX	0.42%	0.68%
Fidelity Tax-Free Money Market Fund www.fidelity.com; 800-343-3548	FMOXX	0.47%	0.46%

[a]Through 10/31/2012

costs substantially. The coverage you really want is against the calamity of being unable to work for years and years. Consider buying coverage only against a major loss.

As with all financial products you buy, shop around. The overarching principle is that the more you pay the provider of the financial service, the less there will be for you.

5. *Diversification reduces anxiety.*

Diversification reduces the risk of any investment program. You should hold not just a few common stocks, but rather a broadly diversified portfolio. You should hold not just U.S. stocks, but also the stocks of foreign countries, including stocks in the fast-growing emerging markets such as China, Brazil, and India. You should hold bonds as well as stocks. While stock markets all over the world tend to go down together during times of financial crisis, broad diversification usually reduces both short-term and long-term risk.

6. *Avoid all credit card debt—period.*

There are few absolute rules in investing except the avoidance of credit card debt. There is no way you can get ahead of the game if you are paying 18, 20, or 22 percent on your outstanding credit card balance. If you do have a credit card balance, the most profitable investment you can make is to pay off your credit card debt, so concentrate your efforts on paying it off.

7. *Ignore the short-term sound and fury of Mr. Market.*

The biggest mistakes investors make are letting emotions dominate and being influenced by the crowd. Investors cause themselves substantial heartache and inferior returns by making buy and sell decisions based on the provocations of Mr. Market and the all-too-human tendency to follow the herd, especially during the inevitable periods of excessive optimism and pessimism. When everyone around you is losing his or her head, just stand there and *do nothing*. Keep your eyes and your mind focused on the long term.

8. *Use low-cost index funds.*

Nobody knows more than the total of all knowledge of all those active and often expert investors who together determine the market prices of stocks. It is true that the market sometimes makes mistakes—often egregious ones such as the overvaluation of high-tech and Internet stocks at the turn of the century. But many of the pundits who predicted the Internet crash had been calling the market "substantially overvalued" in 1992.

Market timers are wrong at least as often as they are right, and when they are wrong, the cost of being wrong is often quite substantial. Yes, the market can and does make mistakes, but don't even try to outsmart it. Over the past 50 years, our securities markets have been transformed from markets dominated almost entirely by individual investors to markets dominated by full-time professional institutional investors. Today, only the most remarkably gifted and diligent individual investors should even begin to consider buying individual stocks in an attempt to beat the market.

We have over 100 years of collective experience, keep up with the professional literature, have taught investing in leading graduate schools, and serve on investment committees all over the world—and we are both glad we index. Most professional investors index a substantial share of their equity and bond portfolios because indexing provides broad diversification at low cost with tax efficiency.

Use index funds for all your long-term investments. With index funds, you don't get average performance. You get above-average performance because index funds have lower expense charges and avoid most unnecessary costs and unnecessary taxes. Later in this chapter, we will recommend the specific funds you could consider.

9. *Focus on major investment categories. Avoid "exotics" like venture capital, private equity, and hedge funds.* We believe you should focus on three simple investment categories: (1) common stocks, which represent ownership interests in manufacturing and service-oriented companies; (2) bonds, which are IOUs of governments, government agencies, and corporations; and (3) real estate, which can best be acquired through your ownership of your own single-family house.

We know that salespeople will regale you with fascinating stories about how certain exotic investments such as hedge funds, commodities, private equity, or venture capital can make you rich, even quickly. Do not listen. Sure, fascinating stories appear in the media from time to time about spectacular profits being made, but here are four good reasons for urging abstinence:

1. Only the very best performers in each exotic category achieve great results.

2. The records of the *average* performers are discouraging, and those in the third and fourth quartiles can be deeply disappointing.

3. The best performers are already fully booked and are not accepting new investors.

4. If you have not already established a clearly preferential position as an investor, your chances of investing with the best are, realistically, *zero*.

If you don't own a large private jet, hobnob with movie stars, and know your way around unusually well, then you can—and should—ignore the exotics. They're not for you or for either of us. Beware! If you look hard enough to find a manager who will assure you that he will do great things for you in one of the exotics, you *will* find him, but don't even begin to think that the promise will actually be fulfilled.

ASSET ALLOCATION

The appropriate allocation for individual investors depends upon a few key factors. The primary factor is age. If you have lots of time to ride out the ups and downs of the market, you can afford a large allocation to common stocks. If you are retired, it's wise to invest conservatively. Another factor is your financial situation. A widow in ill health, who is unable to work and who counts on her investments to cover her living expenses, will not want to risk losing substantial amounts of capital during a stock market downturn. She has neither the time horizon nor the earnings from employment to ride out a major market setback. The third big factor is your temperament. Some people simply can't stand to experience wide swings in their net worth and will want to overweight bonds and cash reserves in their portfolios. Other people care more about long-term growth. To each his own—with caution. Know thyself and match your investing to who you are and where you are in life.

> Know thyself and match your investing
> to who you are and where you are in life.

Thousands of people go skiing on a typical winter's day, and almost all of them have a wonderful time skiing at their own level on the trails and slopes that are right for them. The secret to success and enjoyment in so many parts of life is to know your capabilities and stay within them. Similarly, the key to success in investing is to know yourself and invest within your investing capabilities *and* within your emotional capacities.

No asset allocation will fit all 30-year-olds, 50-year-olds, or 80-year-olds. Even an 80-year-old might want an asset allocation more suitable for a 30-year-old if she plans to leave most of her estate to her children or grandchildren. The appropriate allocation for those planning bequests should be geared to the age of the recipient, not the age of the donor, for that part of their total investments.

The key to success in investing is to invest with the asset mix that's best for you, considering:

- Your financial situation: assets, income, and savings—now and in the future.
- Your age.
- Your emotional strengths—particularly at market highs and market lows—and your attitude toward market risk.
- Your knowledge of and interest in investing.

ASSET ALLOCATION RANGES

Now let's get down to the specifics. Assuming you have already set up your cash reserve, we present our asset allocation guidelines next as reasonable age-related ranges. They will make sense for 90 percent of all investors. Individual circumstances and investment skills and emotional strengths could make allocations outside these ranges appropriate for you, but even so, this is where to start.

We also recommend that you own your house if you can afford to do so. The main reason is to enhance the quality of your living. But putting some of your money into a single-family home will also give you a real estate investment in addition to the stocks and bonds in your savings retirement plan.

> Our asset allocation guidelines . . . show how you might wisely change your asset mix according to your age and your age-related tolerance for market risks.

Here are two tables that show how you might wisely change your asset mix according to your age and your age-related tolerance for market risks. The first table shows what Burt advises. We both agree that this pattern is sensibly conservative for most investors. Charley worries that it may be too conservative and offers an alternative, on page 109, with more exposure to stocks and thus to market volatility, particularly now when the Fed is vigorously depressing interest rates.

Burt's Allocation Ranges for Different Age Groups

Age Group	Percent in Stocks	Percent in Bonds
20–30s	75–90	25–10
40–50s	65–75	35–25
60s	45–65	55–35
70s	35–50	65–50
80s and beyond	20–40	80–60

Charley's Allocation Ranges for Different Age Groups

Age Group	Percent in Stocks	Percent in Bonds
20–30s	100	0
40s	90–100	10–0
50s	75–85	25–15
60s	70–80	30–20
70s	40–60	60–40
80s and beyond	30–50	70–50

Charley's recommended portfolio mix aims for a higher rate of return over the *long* term, but depends crucially on an investor's *short*-term staying power because bad markets are sure to come again and again. Charley points out that most young people don't count their most important "equity"—their personal knowledge capital and the large present value of their future earnings from work. Burt notes that we can also lose our jobs. Both agree strongly that all investors are better safe than sorry and that no investor should take on risks outside his or her comfort zone. Charley's allocations to stocks *assume* indexing, as do Burt's.

We need to emphasize again that the allocation you choose depends critically on your emotional ability to accept big swings in the market value of your portfolio.

Not even your psychiatrist can tell you the proper allocation. If you go toward the 100 percent allocation to common stock investment, as Charley would recommend for young savers, you must be prepared to accept that at times your 401(k) will look like a 301(k) or even a 201(k) when stocks fall sharply. If you can accept that kind of volatility, that's fine. But Burt, who spends a lot of time counseling young faculty members at Princeton, knows how tough it is to see the value of your savings shrink, and that is why he tends to recommend a lower allocation to equities.

For those who are most comfortable with year-to-year market fluctuations, Charley would even favor 100 percent in stocks for younger investors, which is what he is glad he did (and kept doing even into his early seventies). Taking on more market risk by increasing the proportion of stocks in your portfolio will probably result in your earning a greater long-run rate of return. (It could also result in lots more sleepless nights.) If you are not sure you can live with and live all the way through the worst market turbulence, don't take on extra market risk. In the "eat well" versus "sleep well" trade-off, reduce your stock percentage to the level where you know, given who you really are, that you will sleep well.

Put your long-term investments into low-cost index funds. The best choice for your equity investments is a fund indexed to the total world stock market. If you are truly uncomfortable investing in "foreign" stocks, you could choose a domestic total stock market fund. We recommend that you be diversified internationally because the United States represents less than half of the world's economic activity and stock market capitalization. For your bonds, choose a total U.S. bond market index fund.

As you get older, change the mix toward bond investments as the tables indicate. You can usually accomplish this rather easily by changing the allocation of the annual contribution to your 401(k) plan. If adjusting new allocations is insufficient, you could gradually shift some of your existing assets from stocks to bonds.

Once a year, rebalance your portfolio to the stock–bond balance that is right for you. Suppose your preferred allocation is 60 percent stocks and 40 percent bonds, but an exuberant stock market has pushed the equity allocation to 70 percent. Take some of the equity gains off the table and restore your 60–40 balance. (Or, if a punishing bear market reduced the equity proportion to 50 percent, sell some bonds and buy more stocks.) If you have other investments, be sure to do your rebalancing in the tax-sheltered part of your portfolio—your 401(k) or IRA—so you will avoid paying capital gains taxes.

INVESTING IN RETIREMENT

We recommend a substantial allocation to bonds for investors in retirement because bonds provide a relatively steady source of income for living expenses. Some common stocks, however, are included to provide inflation protection, and some TIPS (Treasury inflation protection bonds) are included in a total bond market index fund. The interest paid on TIPS is augmented during periods when the rate of inflation rises, so retirees can expect increases in income during inflationary periods.

Remember the important exception: If you are fortunate enough to have enough capital to be able to meet your living expenses without tapping into your assets, you can choose a different asset allocation more heavily weighted to stocks. Money that you expect to leave to children and grandchildren should be invested according to their age, not yours.

Most people, however, will be drawing down their savings during retirement. They will be faced with a decision of whether to buy an annuity with part or all of their retirement savings. A fixed annuity is a contract with an insurance company. For an initial payment by you, the insurance company will guarantee to pay you a fixed annual amount for as long as you live. Annuities have one important advantage—they ensure that you will not outlive your money. Most financial planners advise retirees to purchase annuities.

There are individual circumstances that argue against annuities, however. Once you die, the payments from the insurance company stop. Thus, if you are in poor health, you may not be well served by an annuity contract. If you have sufficient resources to leave a substantial estate to children and grandchildren, you will not want to purchase an annuity. And fixed annuities have one major disadvantage: Payouts do not increase to offset inflation.

Here is our KISS advice: If you are reasonably healthy as you enter the retirement years (and especially if you have good genes for a long life and few bad risk factors), invest half of your fixed-income investments in an annuity. Then, even if you live to 100, you will never outlive your assets. But, be an educated consumer. Buy only a plain vanilla fixed annuity. The fancy annuities, which adjust for inflation and have all kinds of bells and whistles, may *appear* attractive. But they carry large expense charges and are difficult to analyze. Shop around. In general, you will get a better deal by buying direct from the company rather than by providing commission income for a hungry sales rep.

GETTING SPECIFIC

Here we will list the funds we believe you should use for your common stock and bond investments. All the recommended funds are broad index funds and all are very low cost.

Not all index funds are the same; there are hundreds to choose from. Some equity index funds concentrate on big companies (so-called large capitalization stocks). The Standard & Poor's 500 index fund is such a fund. Other index funds concentrate on smaller companies, or on high-growth stocks, or on particular sectors of the economy, or on foreign companies. There is also a variety of bond index funds, from very safe short-term government bonds to risky indexes of high-yield bonds. We recommend that you concentrate on two broad-based index funds—one a total worldwide stock market fund and the other a total bond market fund.

We offer a choice of broad-based index funds. We do so not because we think you should own more than one fund of each particular type. Both authors have had a long association with the Vanguard Group of Investment Companies, and we wish to avoid even the possible appearance of a conflict of interest.

All the funds listed meet our criterion of having low expense ratios. Our preference for an equity index fund is that you diversify globally. The United States represents only about 40 percent of the world stock market. We buy cars from Japan and Germany; we buy wine from France, Australia, and Chile; and we buy clothing from China, Vietnam, and Indonesia. We believe your stock portfolio should be global as well. If you don't invest in a total world index fund, we recommend that only half of your stock portfolio be invested in a U.S. total stock market index fund, with their other half in a total international stock market index fund.

We also list our recommendations for suitable total U.S. stock market index funds. We recommend "total" stock market funds, rather than the popular index funds based on narrower indexes such as the Standard & Poor's 500 large-company stock index, because the S&P 500 represents only about 70 percent of the total value of all stocks traded in the United States. It excludes the 30 percent made up of smaller companies, many of which are the most entrepreneurial and capable of the fastest future growth.

Any of the funds listed in the table on page 117 would be suitable, but be sure to notice the differences in expense ratios.

Beginning stock market investors should start with a U.S. total stock market fund before adding an international fund. A total U.S. stock market index fund will actually provide some global diversification because many of the multinational "domestic" companies—from General Electric to Coca-Cola—do a great deal of their business abroad. We do believe, however, that investors should combine one of the total U.S. stock market index funds with a total international stock market index fund. The table on page 118 lists our recommendations for suitable total international equity funds.

There is a one-stop shopping method to obtain both domestic and international equity investments in one fund. The fund is called the Total World Stock Index Fund. The expense ratio, cited in the following table, is slightly higher than those of the individual funds listed previously, and there is a small purchase charge. But it

Data on Selected Total U.S. Stock Market Index Funds, 2012

Fund Name	Index	Minimum Sales Charge	Minimum Initial Purchase	Minimum Subsequent Purchase	Recent Expense Ratio	Payroll Deduction?	401(k), IRA Available?
Fidelity Total Market Index, www.fidelity.com; 800-343-3548	Dow/ Wilshire 5000	None	$10,000	$1,000	0.10%	Yes	Yes
Schwab Total 1000 Investor Class, www.schwab.com; 800-435-4000	Custom Index	None	$100	$1	0.29%	Yes	Yes
Vanguard Total Stock Market Index, www.vanguard.com; 800-662-7447	MSCI Broad Market	None	$3,000	$1	0.06%	Yes	Yes

Data on Selected International Stock Market Index Funds, 2012

Fund Name	Ticker	Minimum Sales Charge	Minimum Initial Purchase	Minimum Subsequent Purchase	Recent Expense Ratio	Payroll Deduction?	401(k), IRA Available?
Vanguard Total International Stock Index, www.vanguard.com; 800-662-7447	VGTSX	None	$3,000	$1	0.34%	Yes	Yes
Fidelity Spartan International Index, www.fidelity.com; 800-343-3548	FSIIX	None	$10,000	$1	0.20%	Yes	Yes

Data on Vanguard Total World Stock Index Funds, 2012

Fund Name	Ticker Symbol	Minimum Initial Purchase	Minimum Subsequent Purchase	Recent Expense Ratio	Payroll	401(k), IRA Available?
Vanguard Total World Stock Index, www.vanguard.com; 800-662-7447	VTWSX	$3,000	$1	0.40%	Yes	Yes

Data on Selected Bond Index Funds, 2012

2012 Fund Name	Maximum Sales Charge	Minimum Initial Purchase	Minimum Subsequent Purchase	Recent Expense Ratio	Payroll Deduction?	401(k), IRA Available?
Schwab Total Bond Market Index, www.schwab.com; 800-435-4000	None	$2500	$1	0.58%	Yes	Yes
Vanguard Total Bond Market Index Fund, www.vanguard.com; 800-662-7447	None	$3,000	$100	0.10%	Yes	Yes
Fidelity US Bond Index, www.fidelity.com; 800-343-3548	None	$10,000	$1	0.22%	Yes	Yes

is a convenient way to obtain the broadest diversification in a single fund.

Investing in a Total World Stock Index Fund is a convenient way to obtain the broadest diversification in a single fund . . . like one-stop shopping.

Well-diversified portfolios should have holdings of bonds as well as stocks. Again, we believe that index funds provide the most efficient vehicle for individual investors to hold bonds. On the opposite page, we list three bond index funds that are suitable investments.

We believe that the funds listed here provide suitable exposure to the stock and bond markets. They can easily be purchased by calling the toll-free numbers listed or by visiting the web sites.

Some investors will find that exchange traded funds, or ETFs, will be useful investment instruments. ETFs—most are based on index funds—trade like individual stocks. The two most popular ETFs are the QQQQs (or "cubes") that track the NASDAQ 100 index and the "Spyders" (ticker SPY, which explains the peculiar spelling) that track the Standard & Poor's 500 stock index. Neither of these ETFs is as broad as we would like, but fortunately, new ones are now available that track total stock market indexes in the United States and in the world.

The table on the opposite page shows the menu of ETFs that we recommend. ETFs tend to have very low expense ratios, and they can be more tax efficient than mutual funds because they are able to sell holdings without generating a taxable event. This could be an advantage for taxable investors. However, brokerage commissions are charged on the purchase of ETFs, and for small and moderate purchases these commissions can overwhelm those other advantages. No-load indexed mutual funds typically have no purchase fees. However, if you are investing a lump sum (as, for example, when rolling over an established plan such as an IRA), an ETF may be an optimal choice.

The Vanguard Total World ETF (ticker VT) will give you all the diversification you need, over both domestic and all international markets, with one-stop shopping.

Exchange Traded Funds (ETFs)

	Ticker	Expense Ratio
Total U.S. Stock Market		
iShares Russell 3000	IWV	0.20%
Vanguard Total Stock Market	VTI	0.06%
Total World Ex-U.S.		
Vanguard FTSE All World	VEU	0.18%
SPDR MSCI ACWI	CWI	0.34%
Total World Including U.S.		
Vanguard Total World	VT	0.24%
iShares MSCI ACWI	ACWI	0.34%
Total Bond Market U.S.		
Vanguard Total Bond Market	BND	0.10%
iShares Barclays Aggregate	AGG	0.08%

VI

TIMELESS LESSONS FOR TROUBLED TIMES

Since *Elements* was first written, investors have lived through harrowing economic times, with unprecedented market volatility. Toward the end of the first decade of the 2000s, it appeared to some observers that the financial system was likely to self-destruct and that capitalism was running in reverse. Rather than "the Great Moderation," the label often given to the stability of the preceding period, the faltering economy engendered comparisons with the Great Depression of the 1930s. Many European nations suffered a debt crisis, and the very viability of the Eurozone was widely debated. The stock market lost half of its value. The entire decade was often referred to as "the lost decade" for investors.

It is not surprising, then, that many investors simply abandoned the stock market. The volatility was just too frightening for many people. The stock market seemed to be too risky a place for retirement savings, too unnerving for ordinary investors to handle. Moreover, some professionals, particularly those whose financial interest was enhanced by frequent trading, announced the death of "buy and hold" and proclaimed that the only way to be a successful investor was to "time the market." "Diversification is dead" was another common bromide. "Today's stock markets are too highly correlated," so-called experts said. When markets go down, "there is no place to hide." Small wonder that investors could get thoroughly confused as they listened to this often-conflicted advice.

We disagree. We believe that the timeless investment lessons presented in this book are even more relevant in today's volatile markets. We believe that short-term volatility does not represent real risk for the average investor accumulating a retirement nest egg over many years. Indeed, volatility can be your friend and actually enhance returns for the disciplined long-term investor who is saving regularly, while those investors who attempt market timing all too often make the worst mistakes at the worst times.

Anyone who tries to time the market is usually his own worst enemy. Anxious investors almost invariably do the wrong thing, converting short-term modest losses into long-term permanent losses, resulting in a major investment blunder. The behavior of many investors during market crises convinces us more than ever of the folly of market timing. We've seen it many times. During the Internet Bubble that peaked in early 2000, overly optimistic investors poured their savings into Internet stocks. Just as the financial crisis was at its peak and the stock markets of the world hit bottom in 2008, individuals pulled more money than ever before *out* of the stock market rather than taking advantage of the bargain prices and putting money in. The same happened at the market bottom in 2011 when Europe was the epicenter of the financial meltdown.

Diversification, and the rebalancing strategies we advocate in *Elements*, are time-tested strategies that really do reduce investment risk.* Because we think these time-less lessons are so important during times like this—when markets are unstable and there is such a cacophony of bad advice bombarding the average investor—we have added this brief final chapter.

VOLATILITY AND DOLLAR-COST AVERAGING

The volatility of equity markets can be turned to advantage for savers who are long-term investors who will be accumulating a retirement nest egg over time through periodic investments—such as individuals with 401(k) plans. These investors will be taking advantage of the dollar-cost averaging described in Chapter III. In introducing this simple, time-tested technique, we showed that a patient investor can actually build up a larger retirement fund in a volatile flat market than in a market that is continuously rising.

Moving from the hypothetical calculations shown earlier, here's an actual illustration of how the strategy of consistent

---

* We indicate later, however, that diversification strategies need some fine-tuning.

investment in equities can produce a growing retirement fund—even when the stock seems to simply tread water for a period of a decade or more. The first decade of the 2000s was one of the toughest investment decades in history. Early in the decade, the market suffered a 50 percent decline as the Internet Bubble of the late 1990s burst. Later in the decade, the global financial crisis wreaked havoc on investors as stock prices declined by almost 50 percent *again*. At the end of 2010, the stock market index, as measured by the Standard and Poor's (S&P) 500 stock index, was actually lower than it was at the beginning of the decade in January 2000. This kind of experience soured millions of Americans on investing in stocks. But was it really so bad for savers who followed the rules we espouse?

In the following illustration, we assume that the investor starts her program in January 2000. Her timing was perfectly terrible since market prices then were at a historical peak. But despite losing about half of her initial investment, she has the self-discipline, clarity of purpose, and perseverance to continue to invest in each and every period—"good" times and "bad." To keep the calculations simple we assume that $1,000 per year is invested and that the investment is made only once a year on the first trading day of January. We also assume that dividends are reinvested. The table below uses actual values for the S&P 500 stock index.

The remarkable conclusion is that even during a decade that was disastrous for many equity investors, our dollar-cost averaging investor enjoyed a moderate positive return and was able to enhance the final value of her retirement nest egg. We believe that equity markets will continue to exhibit substantial short-term volatility in the future. For the long-term investors, that short-term volatility may be an annoyance, but it is not a major problem: It's an

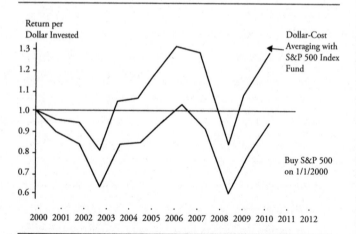

Dollar-Cost Averaging During the "Lost Decade"

opportunity. Long-term investors can and should look beyond the inevitable market ups and downs. The major risk for long-term investors hoping to enjoy a comfortable retirement is *not* having to endure the ups and downs of stock prices; the risk for long-term investors is letting the volatility of the markets keep them from a regular program of buying equities. Dollar-cost averaging is one of the long-term investor's four best friends.

DIVERSIFICATION IS STILL A TIME-HONORED STRATEGY TO REDUCE RISK

Diversification is the time-honored way to reduce investment risk. Diversification is as basic to successful investing as good health is to a great life. The general idea is to include in your portfolio some asset types that provide a degree of stability during the inevitable equity bear markets. But even diversification has been challenged during the recent difficult times in the stock market. There are, of course, a few kernels of truth in arguments of the "naysayers" who say that diversification fails us just when we need it most. Stock markets in different national markets *have* become much more highly correlated. Globalization *has* tended to make the stock markets in different countries go up and down together. Abrupt market declines around the world *are* more synchronous. Despite the plausibility of these arguments, diversification remains an extraordinarily useful technique to achieve your investment goals. Diversification is another one of the long-term investor's best friends.

First, not all financial assets go up and down together. For example, bond prices have often risen when stock prices fell. If a recession is expected, corporate earnings can be expected to decline, so stock prices are likely to fall. But the monetary authorities typically try to reduce the severity of the recession by lowering interest rates, and when rates fall, bond prices rise. Thus bonds often zig just when stock prices zag, imparting a degree of stability to your overall portfolio. In fact, in recent years, returns from stocks and bonds have tended to move in opposite directions. (Later in the chapter we have more to say about bonds in the current environment.)

Moreover, even when equity markets around the world tend to move up and down almost in unison, there have been vast differences in the performance of different stock markets. While the short-term fluctuations in developed and emerging equity markets were almost perfectly correlated during the first decade of the 2000s, the long-term performance of those markets was vastly different. Developed markets were basically flat during the decade, producing a minuscule rate of return, but emerging markets produced an overall return for investors of 10 percent per year compounded.

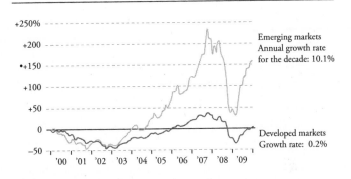

Diversification into Emerging Markets Helped during the Lost Decade

Sources: MSCI and Bloomberg.

REBALANCING

We want to reemphasize that the timeless lesson of rebalancing covered in Chapter III proved its value very well—especially during the most volatile periods of the market. Recall that rebalancing simply means that periodically, such as once a year, you look at the asset allocation of your portfolio and bring it back into the kind of balance that makes you comfortable. For example, suppose you are a "nervous Nelson" and prefer not to have equities be more than 50 percent of your portfolio—with bonds comprising the other half. Rebalancing says simply that if equity prices rise and bond prices fall, so that your portfolio has become 70 percent stocks and 30 percent bonds, you should sell some stocks and buy some bonds to restore the balance you desire, because it's consistent with the risk level that is right for you.

The chart on page 137 demonstrates the benefits of rebalancing a 60–40, stock–bond portfolio. Notice that annual rebalancing added almost 1½ percentage points of return per year over a 15-year period—*and* the stability of the annual return improved as well. You may wonder what alchemy could have improved the return so much. The answer is that rebalancing makes you take some profits in the asset class that has done particularly well and invest in the one that has become a better bargain.

If you think of what was happening to markets over the period, it is very clear why the technique worked so well. The rebalancing was done every January. In January 2000, no one knew that the Internet Bubble would burst in March of that year. But you did know that the equity prices had risen sharply in the market euphoria and that rising interest rates were causing bond prices to fall. So the unintended allocation in January had become close to 75 percent stocks and 25 percent bonds rather than the intended 60–40 mix. To rebalance, some stocks were sold and the money invested in bonds to restore the balance. Now think of January 2003—after the market had tumbled sharply and interest rates had fallen, leading to rising bond prices. No one knew that the stock market had made a bottom in October 2002, but you would have seen that bonds were then 55 percent of the portfolio, well above the target allocation. So bonds were sold and stocks were bought. During the global financial crisis, toward the end of the first decade of the 2000s, rebalancing again worked for you. Interest rates had been driven down to near zero on Treasury securities, so the portfolio in January 2009 had become overweighted with bonds and underweighted with equities. It was time to rebalance again.

What rebalancing forces you to do is the very opposite of what most investors do. Most investors tend to buy at market tops when everyone is optimistic and sell at the bottom when it appears that the sky is falling. (That is, of course, what creates market tops and bottoms.) Rebalancing forces you to do the opposite. Disciplined rebalancing is another of the long-term investor's best friends.

DIVERSIFICATION AND REBALANCING TOGETHER

Burt has for years proposed* for an investor in his or her 50s a diversified portfolio of 33 percent bonds, 33 percent U.S. stocks, 17 percent foreign developed market stocks, and 17 percent emerging market stocks. (This was meant to be only a rough guideline.) All investors are different in their capacity for taking risk and their willingness to assume it. Charley's view is that a starting point would be only a 20 percent allocation to bonds. Whatever the allocation, the rebalancing strategy we both recommend would produce the same kind of benefits shown in the illustration that follows. The chart shows the performance of Burt's portfolio contrasted with a nondiversified purely U.S. domestic stock portfolio. The undiversified domestic

---

* See his *A Random Walk Down Wall Street*, 10th ed. (paper, New York: W.W. Norton, 2012).

portfolio was basically flat throughout the "lost" first decade of the 2000s. But the diversified portfolio, annually rebalanced, despite the very poor performance of the stock markets in the major developed countries of the world, almost doubled in value.

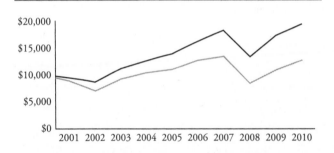

Advantages of Diversification and Rebalancing

Source: Vanguard and Morningstar.

INDEX AT LEAST THE CORE OF YOUR PORTFOLIO

The difficult market environment since the first edition of *Elements* also reinforces for us the message of Chapter II—use index funds for most, if not all, of your portfolio of financial assets. "Beating the market," of course, means outperforming the consensus of many hardworking and well-informed professional competitors. Changes in the market—due to changes in market participants—have been substantial, particularly in the aggregate. Over the past 50 years, trading volume has increased 2,000 times— from 2 million shares a day to 4 billion—while the dollar value of derivatives traded (options, swap contracts, etc.) in value traded, has gone from zero to even more than the primary markets in stocks and bonds.

Most importantly, the worldwide increase in the number of highly trained experts working intensively to achieve any competitive advantage has been phenomenal. The enormous increase in competition by several hundred thousand well-informed, tech-savvy, hardworking professionals at the world's major institutions has surely made it increasingly difficult for any one investor to outperform the market benchmark. As a result, like a gigantic prediction market, today's stock market expresses all of the expert estimates of value coming every day from an extraordinary number of independent, experienced, and competitive decision makers. Against this consensus of experts, any manager of a diversified portfolio of publicly traded securities is deeply challenged. Extensive, undeniable data show how improbable it is that any particular investment manager can be identified *in advance* who will—after costs, taxes, and the fees now charged—achieve the Holy Grail of beating the market. Yes, Virginia, there have been a very few managers who have beaten the market over time, but nobody has found a reliable way of determining *in advance* which specific managers will be the lucky ones.

Over the long run, it has become increasingly hard to beat the market—ironically because so many professional investors who now dominate the markets are so very capable! And it's even harder to determine in advance which fund managers will beat the market. That's why index funds that accept the collective judgment of the experts continue to outperform two-thirds of actively managed funds, and the one-third who appear to be winners in one period are not the same managers who outperform in the next period. Moreover, the underperformers fall short by *twice* as much as the winners outperform.

Critics often say that today's volatile markets demand active management and that management fees are low. Don't believe them. Fees charged by investment managers have increased substantially over the past 50 years—more than fourfold for both institutional investors and individual investors. Yet investment results have *not* improved.

If the upward trend of fees and the downward trend of prospects for beat-the-market performance wave a warning flag for investors—as they certainly should—objective reality should cause all investors who have been believing that investment management fees are *low* to reconsider. Seen in the right perspective, active management fees are *not* low. Fees are *high*—very high.

Of course, when stated as a percent of *assets,* fees do *look* low—a little over 1 percent of assets for individuals. But the investors already own those assets, so investment management fees should really be based on what the investors are getting in the *returns* managers can produce. Calculated correctly as a percentage of *returns*, fees no longer look "low." Do the math. If overall stock returns average, say, 7 percent a year, then those same fees are not 1 percent. They are much higher—over 14 percent for individual investors in mutual funds.

But even this recalculation substantially understates the *real* cost of active beat-the-market investment management. Here's why: Broad-based index funds and exchange-traded funds that reliably produce the market rate of return—with no more than market risk—are now available with even lower fees than when the first edition of *Elements* was published. Today, market-matching returns are available to all investors at low "commodity" prices, such as 5 basis points (5/100 of 1 percent). Therefore, investors should consider the fees charged by active managers not as a percentage of total returns, but as the *incremental* fee for active management as a percentage of the *incremental* risk-adjusted returns *above the market index.*

Thus correctly stated, management fees are quite *high.* Leaving aside several interesting quibbles—such as that, for individual investors, taxes on short-term gains with 100 percent portfolio turnover can be significant—fees are remarkably high. *Incremental* fees are somewhere between 50 percent of *incremental* returns and, amazingly, *infinity* for the majority of fund managers who do not beat the market. And fees are generally closer to the high end than the low end of that range. Are fees for any other services of any kind at such a high proportion of value?

Fees are not "everything," but just as surely, investment management fees are not almost "nothing." And the one thing about investing we can be absolutely sure of is that the higher the fee paid to the purveyor of any investment product, the less there will be for the investor. Fees are far more important than many investors seem to realize. No wonder increasing numbers of individual and institutional investors are turning to indexed ETFs and index mutual funds—and those investors with experience with either or both are steadily increasing their use.

Of course, the mutual fund industry, which thrives on high-fee, actively managed funds, will always be trumpeting the benefits of switching into funds with the best recent "performance." Often you will see advertisements that suggest that you will be better off switching into funds with four- or five-star Morningstar ratings, despite Morningstar's acknowledgment that its star ratings do *not* predict future performance and the reality that simply ranking funds by expense ratio provides a better predictor of future returns. In fact, Morningstar studied the behavior of mutual funds investors from 2000 through 2011 and found that investors lost billions through their return-chasing behavior. Had they simply bought and held a broad-based index fund, they would have improved their returns by almost two percentage points every year.

FINE-TUNING A BOND DIVERSIFICATION STRATEGY

In the first edition of *Elements*, we urged investors to diversify their equity investments by including asset classes in their portfolios that may be relatively uncorrelated with the stock market. Over the 2000s, bonds have been an excellent diversifier, providing stability to portfolio returns by performing particularly well when the stock market declined. But today, bond yields are extraordinarily low. We believe we are in an era now when many bond investors will likely experience very unsatisfactory investment results with many types of bonds. So investors who feel they need the steady income of bonds will have to think very carefully about how they structure their income-producing portfolios.

Unfortunately, we are very likely to be in an era of "financial repression" for some time to come, where savers who invest in ultra-safe fixed-income instruments will receive seriously inadequate returns. Many of the developed economies of the world are burdened with excessive debt. Governments around the world are having great difficulty reining in spending. The seemingly "less painful" policy response to the problem is a deliberate attempt to force savers to accept returns below the rate of inflation for a considerable period of time as the real burdens of debt are reduced. Such financial repression is a subtle form of debt restructuring and represents a type of invisible taxation. Today, the 10-year U.S. Treasury bond yields well under 2 percent, a rate below the headline rate of inflation. Even if inflation over the next decade averages only 2 percent, the rate of the informal Fed target, investors will find that they will have earned less than a *zero* real rate of return. And if inflation accelerates, the rate of current return to investors will be even more *negative*. Moreover, bond prices will fall, compounding the investor's losses.

We have seen this movie before. After World War II, America found itself with a debt/GDP ratio over 100 percent—close to today's level. The government's postwar policy response was to keep interest rates pegged at the low wartime levels for several years—10-Year Treasuries yielded 2½ percent during the late 1940s—and then allow them to rise gradually beginning in the early 1950s. Not only were interest rates artificially low at the start of the period, but bondholders suffered capital losses when interest rates were allowed to rise. Inflation reduced the debt/GDP ratio to about one-third in 1980, but at the expense of the bondholders, who suffered a double whammy during the period. As a result, even bondholders who held to maturity received *nominal* rates of return that were barely positive over the period, while *real* returns (after inflation) were significantly negative. As interest rates doubled, and then doubled again, bondholders suffered substantial capital losses. We are likely entering a similar period today with the result being a real harm to bond-holding investors.

So what is an investor—especially an investor in retirement who wants steady income—to do? Investors should consider two reasonable strategies. The first is to look for bonds with moderate credit risk, but with higher yields than U.S. Treasuries. The second is to consider substituting a portfolio of dividend-paying blue-chip stocks for a high-quality bond portfolio.

Whereas long-term U.S. Treasury bonds are likely to be sure losers for investors today, not all bonds should be considered bad like "four-letter words." There are some classes of bonds where yield spreads over Treasuries are reasonably attractive. One category is tax-exempt municipal bonds. The fiscal problems of state and local governments are well known, and the parlous state of municipal budgets has led to very-high-yield spreads on all tax-exempt bonds. Many revenue bonds with stable and growing sources of revenue sell at quite attractive yields relative to U.S. Treasuries. For example, the

New York/New Jersey Port Authority gets reliable revenues from airports, bridges, and tunnels to support its debt. Long-term Port Authority bonds yielded close to 5 percent in 2012, and they are free of both federal and state and local taxes in the states in which they operate. (High-yielding diversified portfolios of tax-exempt bonds are available through closed-end investment companies. While these funds employ moderate leverage, they provided yields around 6 percent. If tax rates increase in the future, they will become even more attractive as investments.)

Foreign bonds in countries that have much better fiscal balances than we have in the United States can be attractive today. An example would be Australia, where high-quality bond yields are in the high single digits. Australia has a low debt/GDP ratio (about 25 percent), a relatively young population, and abundant natural resources, making its future economic prospects bright. Its currency has been appreciating against the U.S. dollar. High-quality Australian bonds were available at yields of around 8 percent in early 2012. The same arguments can be made for Brazil and other emerging markets. Diversified portfolios of high-quality emerging market bonds are available in early 2012 at yields well above those in the United States.

A second strategy would be to substitute a portfolio of blue-chip stocks with generous dividends for an equivalent high-quality U.S. bond portfolio. Many excellent U.S. common stocks have dividend yields that compare very favorably with the bonds issued by the same companies—and their dividends are likely to rise steadily in the future. One example would be AT&T. AT&T stock yields close to 5 percent—almost double the yield on 10-year AT&T bonds. And AT&T has raised its dividend at a compound annual growth rate of 5 percent for 35 years. Bond interest payments are fixed. If inflation accelerates, so should AT&T's earnings and dividends, making the stock perhaps even less risky than the bond. We believe income-seeking investors will be better off owning a portfolio of high-dividend-paying stocks than by holding a portfolio of bonds in the same companies. The following exhibit compares the yields available from a standard, diversified bond portfolio with a portfolio of dividend-paying stocks and emerging-market bonds, where interest rates are sufficiently high to compensate for expected inflation.

Surrogate Bond Portfolios in the Age of Financial Repression

	Yield Late 2012
I. Regular Bond Portfolio	
Vanguard Total Bond Market ETF (BND)	2.9%
II. Surrogate Bond Portfolio	
Emerging Market Bond ETF (EMB)	4.7%
Vanguard Equity Income Fund (VEIRX)	2.9%
Average	3.8%

Note that a broadly diversified "Total Bond Market" portfolio, available as the ETF ticker BND, yielded less than 3 percent as of the start of 2012. A surrogate portfolio made up of one-half broadly diversified emerging market bonds and one-half a fund of dividend-paying stocks yielded about 3.8 percent. And the dividend yield of the stock fund is likely to rise over time.

A FINAL THOUGHT

We can be certain that many more surprises will be in store for investors in the future and that our securities markets will remain volatile. The investors who will lose are those who chase after the current "hot" stock or the recently "best" mutual fund and then panic and sell out at times of adversity. The long-term winners will be those who control the one thing they can control—their investment costs—and have the fortitude to tolerate short-term volatility and stay the course in following a sensible long-run investment program.

Long-term investors will achieve the best results by capitalizing on the four best friends of the serious long-term investor:

- Diversification
- Rebalancing
- Dollar-cost averaging
- Indexing

Patience and persistence are the key factors for success in investing. The long-term investor who uses these tools and sticks with a sensible long-run investment program will have the best success.

A SUPER
SIMPLE SUMMARY:
KISS INVESTING

The steps to a comfortable, care-free retirement are really simple, but they require discipline and emotional fortitude.

1. Save regularly and start early.
2. Use company- and government-sponsored retirement plans to supercharge your savings and minimize your taxes.

3. Diversify broadly over different securities with low-cost "total market" index funds and different asset types.

4. Rebalance annually to the asset mix that's right for you.

5. Stay the course and ignore market fluctuations; they are likely to lead to serious and costly investing mistakes. Focus on the long term.

KISS investing—Keep It Simple, Sweetheart—is the best and easiest and lowest cost and worry-free way to invest for retirement security. Go for it!

Speaking of sweethearts, all wives and all husbands should be sure they both know *all* the facts about their investments. And because we are each different in our emotions about investments, markets, and money, families should strive again and again to share their thoughts and feelings so they can understand each other and make decisions together.

APPENDIX:
SAVE ON
TAXES LEGALLY

Because the U.S. government wants to encourage us to save more, a variety of retirement plans are available that allow individual taxpayers to deduct from their federal taxes every dollar they save. Moreover, these plans allow the earnings and gains from these savings plans to compound over time tax free. Here we describe the details of these tax-advantaged plans. This section is, by necessity, more detailed and dryer than most readers would like. You can skip it if you wish. Just make sure you are taking full advantage of at least one of these plans. They not only permit you to save more but also let the earnings from your savings compound at a faster rate.

INDIVIDUAL RETIREMENT ACCOUNTS (IRAs)

The simplest form of savings and retirement plan available to everyone is the individual retirement account. All people with earnings from employment can take $5,500 a year ($6,500 if you are over 50 years of age) and invest it in a mutual fund or other investment vehicle.* If your income is moderate, you can deduct the entire $5,500 from your taxable income. Thus, if you are in the 28 percent tax bracket, the $5,500 contribution really costs you only $3,960 because your tax bill will go down by $1,540. Moreover, all the earnings from that $5,500 investment will accrue tax free. Wealthier individuals cannot get the same initial tax deduction, but

---

*These are the rules as of 2013; the dollar limits may well be raised in subsequent years.

they do enjoy the benefits of the tax deferral from the investment earnings on their IRA investment account. The result is that the government subsidizes your savings.

Now suppose that you have entered the workforce at age 23 and that you invest $5,000 each year over a 45-year period. Let's further assume that you invest in a broadly diversified mutual fund earning 8 percent per year. No taxes are paid on those earnings until you withdraw the money during retirement. A person who followed such a program of IRA savings would have a final value of over $2 million. The same savings *without* the IRA benefit (with all earnings taxed at a 28 percent rate) total only about $750,000. Even after paying taxes at a 28 percent rate when you withdraw your IRA contribution, you would end up with almost $1.5 million, and you might be in a lower tax bracket during retirement. The figure on page 156 shows the dramatic advantage of investing through a tax-advantaged plan.

You don't have to win the lottery to be a millionaire. Anyone with the will power to save regularly and start early can become a millionaire.

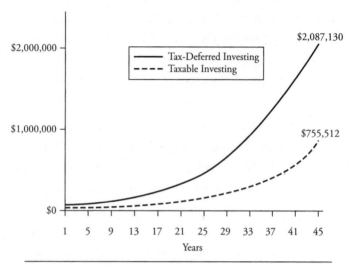

How Tax-Deferred Investing Grows Faster Than Taxable Investing ($5,000 Invested per Year Earning 8 percent)

ROTH IRAs

A type of IRA, called a Roth IRA, is available to savers whose income is below certain levels. (Any mutual fund company can tell you if you qualify.) The traditional IRA lets you deduct your contribution from your taxes immediately—in effect, giving you "jam today." The money gets taxed at retirement when you take the accumulations out. The Roth IRA offers you "jam tomorrow." There is no upfront tax deduction, but when you take the money out, you pay no taxes at all.

You are also allowed to "Roth and Roll." You can roll the balance of your traditional IRA into a Roth, again if your income level qualifies.* You need to pay tax on the amount converted, but from then on neither the earnings nor the withdrawals in retirement are taxed. Moreover, you are not required to take the money out at retirement, and contributions can continue to be made into your seventies and eighties if you wish. Thus, significant amounts can be accumulated tax free for future generations.

The decision of which IRA is best for you can be tough. It depends on such things as whether your tax bracket is likely to be higher or lower in retirement and whether you have sufficient funds in addition to your IRA contribution to pay your income taxes. Most mutual fund companies have "Roth analyzers" that are easy to use. As a rule of thumb, if you are in a low tax bracket now and you are far from retirement, you are very likely to come

---

*In 2012, conversions to a Roth IRA are allowed for all individuals, regardless of income.

out better with a Roth. And if your income is too high to take a tax deduction on a traditional IRA, but low enough to qualify for a Roth, a Roth is certainly the correct choice since your contributions are made after tax in any event.

PENSION PLANS

Retirement plans are available from most employers, and the self-employed can set up their own plans. Most employers now have 401(k) plans; educational institutions have similar 403(b) retirement plans. These are ideal savings vehicles because the money comes out of your salary *before* you even see it and get tempted to spend it. Even better, many employers match the savings you put in with company contributions so that every dollar you save gets multiplied. As of 2013, you can contribute $17,500 per year into such retirement plans, and the contributions do not count as taxable income. If you are over 50 and you need to play "catch up" on your retirement savings, $22,000 per year can be put into the plan.

Self-employed people from Avon ladies to doctors can set up Keogh plans to which they can contribute 20 percent of their income up to $49,000 annually as of 2009. Money paid into the plan is tax deductible, and earnings from the investments are not taxed until they are withdrawn. Even if you have a 401(k) plan at your place of employment, moonlighting income qualifies for this additional plan. Mutual fund companies can help you prepare all the necessary paperwork, as well as advise you on other similar self-directed retirement plans.

By "self-directed," we mean that you can choose any mutual funds you like for the investment of your retirement savings. These plans are a perfectly legal way to checkmate the IRS. You will be making a big mistake if you don't save as much as you possibly can through these tax-sheltered means. If you have any further questions about these plans, you can get brochures from the IRS that cover all the detailed regulations.

We understand that many people already struggling to make ends meet will be unwilling or feel unable to make the sacrifices necessary to take advantage of all the opportunities available. Here's how we believe you ought to prioritize the available vehicles so that you build up as much wealth as possible for your retirement years free from worries about money.

First, contribute to your employer's 401(k) or 403(b) plan up to the limit that will be matched by your employer. Thus, if your employer will match $5,000 of your contributions, you get $10,000 of retirement savings when you contribute your $5,000—double what you put in yourself. Use up any other savings you have for living expenses so you can contribute at least up to the employer matching amount. When you consider that these contributions are not taxed, you can easily see that this is one of the few "free lunches" that will ever be offered to you.

Second, contribute voluntarily up to the maximum that is allowed in your 401(k) plan. Then start an IRA. Even if you don't get an immediate tax deduction, the ability of your investment earnings to compound tax free is an enormous benefit, as the figure on page 156 makes clear.

You should know that there are some disadvantages to these tax-advantaged retirement vehicles. You are not allowed to withdraw money before age 59½, unless you become disabled. If you do withdraw the funds early, you must pay a penalty of 10 percent as well as applicable income taxes. Moreover, any withdrawals will not receive the benefit of future tax-free compounding. You have to keep the retirement kitty invested in the plan. In our view, this is actually an important advantage of the tax system because it so strongly encourages thrift and staying the course. In this case, the tax system encourages us to do something that is truly in our own best interest.

TAX-ADVANTAGED SAVING FOR EDUCATION

A variety of tax-advantaged plans provide incentives for putting money aside for future education expenditures. The most popular are the so-called 529 College Savings Accounts. These accounts allow parents and grandparents to give gifts to children that can be invested for future qualified higher-educational purposes. The plan allows an individual donor to contribute up to $55,000 into a 529 plan. No gift taxes need be paid and estate-tax credits are not affected. All the earnings from the investments in the plan compound tax free. Two parents can contribute $55,000 each, and if there are four well-off grandparents, as much as $330,000 can be contributed to junior's college education. Even with tuitions rising rapidly, the 529 plan, with investment earnings untaxed, can make even the most expensive private college comfortably affordable. If you have kids or grandchildren and can afford to contribute, the 529 plan is an attractive no-brainer.

Some pitfalls to these plans need to be considered. If the funds are not used for qualified expenditures, withdrawals are subject to both income taxes and a 10 percent penalty tax. Some of these plans carry very high expense ratios, so be an educated consumer and shop around to find a low-expense plan.

These plans are sanctioned by individual states, and some states (such as New York) allow you to take a tax deduction for at least part of your contribution. If your state does, too, find a specific plan sanctioned by your state.* Finally, if you are establishing a plan

---

*Comprehensive information on 529 and other education savings plans can be found at www.savingforcollege.com.

for a teenager, for whom college is only a few years away, you may well want the money invested in a short-term bond fund. Money that will be needed for expenditure fairly soon should *not* be invested in the stock market.

RECOMMENDED READING

If you'd like to learn more about investing, these are the books we recommend:

John C. Bogle, *Common Sense on Mutual Funds: New Imperatives for the Intelligent Investor* (John Wiley & Sons, 2000).

John C. Bogle, *The Little Book of Common Sense Investing: The Only Way to Guarantee Your Fair Share of Stock Market Returns* (John Wiley & Sons, 2007).

Jonathan Clements, *25 Myths You've Got to Avoid—If You Want to Manage Your Money Right: The New Rules for Financial Success* (Fireside, 1999).

Charles D. Ellis, *Winning the Loser's Game; Timeless Strategies for Successful Investing*, fifth edition (McGraw-Hill, 2009).

Benjamin Graham, *The Intelligent Investor: The Definitive Book on Value Investing. A Book of Practical Counsel*, with commentary by *Jason Zweig* (HarperBusiness, 2003).

Burton G. Malkiel, *A Random Walk Down Wall Street: The Time-Tested Strategy for Successful Investing*, tenth edition (W. W. Norton & Co., 2012).

David F. Swensen, *Unconventional Success: A Fundamental Approach to Personal Investment* (The Free Press, 2005).

David F. Swensen, *Pioneering Portfolio Management: An Unconventional Approach to Institutional Investment*, fully revised and updated (The Free Press, 2009).

Andrew Tobias, *The Only Investment Guide You'll Ever Need* (Harvest Books, 2005).

Jason Zweig, *Your Money and Your Brain: How the New Science of Neuroeconomics Can Help Make You Rich* (Simon & Schuster, 2008).

ACKNOWLEDGMENTS

William S. Rukeyser, editor extraordinaire, used his deft skills to clarify and simplify every page. On behalf of all readers, thank you, Bill.

We also salute our wonderful wives, Nancy Weiss Malkiel and Linda Koch Lorimer. Vanessa Mobley, Meg Freeborn, and Bill Falloon provided perceptive questions and many helpful suggestions. Ellen DiPippo, Catharine Fortin, and Kimberly Breed made vital contributions by turning our illegible scribbles into readable copy.

Thanks to the Center for Economic Policy Studies at Princeton University for financial support.

Finally, many, many thanks to our students, teachers, and friends in the investment profession who, lucky us, have included Peter Bernstein, Jack Bogle, Warren Buffett, David Dodd, Ben Graham, Tad Jeffrey, Marty Leibowitz, Jay Light, Charlie Munger, Roger Murray, John Neff, Paul Samuelson, Gus Sauter, Bill Sharpe, and David Swensen.

ABOUT THE AUTHORS

BURTON G. MALKIEL

Burton G. Malkiel is the Chemical Bank Emeritus Chairman's Professor of Economics at Princeton University and the author of the bestselling *A Random Walk Down Wall Street*. Malkiel has served as a member of the President's Council of Economic Advisers, Dean of the Yale School of Management, Chair of Princeton's Economics Department, and director of major corporations.

CHARLES D. ELLIS

Charles D. Ellis is a consultant to large public and private institutional investors. He was for three decades managing partner of Greenwich Associates, the international business strategy consulting firm. He serves as Chair of Whitehead Institute, was a director of Vanguard, chair of Yale's investment committee and trustee of the university, and is a trustee and chairs the finance committee at the Robert Wood Johnson Foundation. He has taught the advance investment courses at both Harvard Business School and Yale School of Management, and is the author of 14 books, including the bestselling *Winning the Loser's Game.*

INDEX